Uncharted Leadership is an incredible develop[...] your ability to adapt and lead through tumultuous times. Dr. Angie Ward is a leadership and ministry expert who uses real-life case studies to draw insightful conclusions and stretch our thinking. Whether you use this book on your own or (even better!) with your team, you will walk away a stronger and more effective leader.

—**Kadi Cole**, leadership consultant; executive coach; author,
Developing Female Leaders (www.kadicole.com)

Angie Ward has provided a stunning reference book for ministry leaders in *Uncharted Leadership*. She provides detailed case studies for any situation a ministry leader might encounter. She also provides helpful questions, commentary, updates that change your point of view, and resources for that particular issue. Leadership can be isolating and is becoming more difficult in rapidly changing times, but Angie is once again a trusted voice of wisdom, providing a rich resource to help us navigate.

—**Steve Cuss**, lead pastor, Discovery Christian Church, Denver,
Colorado; author, *Managing Leadership Anxiety: Yours and Theirs*

Through the years, Angie Ward has been an inquisitive, thoughtful, and insightful writer, providing leaders with proven, practical understanding. In *Uncharted Leadership*, Angie again delivers with case studies from which entire teams will benefit through chapter-by-chapter review and topical discussion. Pastors who wish to lead churches out of stagnation or the management of decline need to leave behind twentieth-century metrics and position themselves today with tomorrow in mind. If that's your need or desire, this book can help.

—**Mark DeYmaz**, directional leader, Mosaic Church of Central
Arkansas and Mosaix Global Network; author, *Building a Healthy
Multiethnic Church* and *The Coming Revolution in Church Economics*

Angie Ward has made a significant contribution to leadership studies. Looking back on twenty years of teaching leadership at a seminary, I wish I had such a resource to prepare my students for the realities of ministry. *Uncharted Leadership* also would have been a great help for my years as a pastoral leader. To survive and succeed, especially in these times, leaders need the guidance of these case studies. The questions and commentary invite the reader to engage and wrestle with each one. There is so much wisdom in the core themes Ward identifies in the conclusion. This is a necessary read for anyone courageous enough to step into ministry and determined to create and sustain a healthy environment.

–**John E. Johnson**, associate professor of pastoral theology, Western Seminary; author, *Rooted Leadership: Seeking God's Answers to the Eleven Core Questions Every Leader Faces*

As Angie points out early in this book, classrooms cannot fully prepare us for the joys, pitfalls, and challenges of leadership. At some point, we all find ourselves wishing we could have "known then what we know now." This important book will fast-forward your leadership perspective by placing in your hands the invaluable gift of others' experiences. Each page provides timely insights and ground-level applications every leader needs to move forward with confidence and clarity.

–**Meredith King**, author, *Immovable: Reflections to Build Your Life and Leadership on Solid Ground*; founder, True to Life Ministries; leadership and nonprofit strategist

This is an immensely practical book on adaptive leadership. Dr. Ward brilliantly weaves real-life, thought-provoking case studies together with compelling questions that guide readers to clarify their own values for addressing adaptive leadership challenges. For newer and seasoned leaders alike, *Uncharted Leadership* is an excellent resource for honing one's adaptive-leadership skills.

–**Lisa Rodriguez-Watson**, national director, Missio Alliance

Dr. Angie Ward's new book, *Uncharted Leadership*, takes a unique approach to leadership in the church. Rather than the usual "look how I lead" or "here's some great leadership advice" perspectives, Dr. Ward presents true-to-life examples of leadership crises in church settings and then lets the reader wrestle with the implications. It is an engaging and thought-provoking approach, similar to a pilot spending time in a flight simulator. I highly recommend *Uncharted Leadership* for people just entering ministry and for seasoned ministry professionals looking to grow in their leadership.

—Geoff Surratt, founder, Ministry Together

Every pastor, elder, deacon, and ministry leader needs to read *Uncharted Leadership*. Angie Ward takes the reader on a journey through twenty real-life, messy church scenarios and then a series of crucial questions that help teams make biblical, God-honoring decisions to help the church flourish instead of self-destruct. This book comes at the perfect time after years of complexity and chaos. Think you are good at asking critical questions? *Uncharted Leadership* will take you to the next level. It helped our entire pastoral team become better critical thinkers and question askers.

—Judy West, pastor, staff, and leadership at The Crossing (a multisite church in St. Louis); leader of WXP (Women's Executive Pastor) Network

Uncharted Leadership is a valuable tool to help potential leaders navigate the challenges that often come with leading. This book gives us a front-row seat to learn from others through twenty invaluable case studies that will help anyone seeking to be a successful and impactful leader go farther, faster.

—Carrie Williams, CEO, Leadership Network

UNCHARTED
LEADERSHIP

UNCHARTED
LEADERSHIP

20 CASE STUDIES
TO HELP MINISTRY LEADERS
ADAPT TO UNCERTAINTY

ANGIE WARD

**ZONDERVAN
REFLECTIVE**

ZONDERVAN REFLECTIVE

Uncharted Leadership
Copyright © 2023 by Angie Ward

Requests for information should be addressed to:
Zondervan, *3900 Sparks Dr. SE, Grand Rapids, Michigan 49546*

Zondervan titles may be purchased in bulk for educational, business, fundraising, or sales promotional use. For information, please email SpecialMarkets@Zondervan.com.

ISBN 978-0-310-14342-0 (audio)

Library of Congress Cataloging-in-Publication Data

Names: Ward, Angie, 1970– author.
Title: Uncharted leadership : 20 case studies to help ministry leaders adapt to uncertainty / Angie Ward.
Description: Grand Rapids : Zondervan, 2023. | Includes bibliographical references and index.
Identifiers: LCCN 2023000835 (print) | LCCN 2023000836 (ebook) | ISBN 9780310143031 (paperback) | ISBN 9780310143413 (ebook)
Subjects: LCSH: Christian leadership. | Leadership—Case studies. | BISAC: RELIGION / Christian Living / Leadership & Mentoring | RELIGION / Christian Ministry / Pastoral Resources
Classification: LCC BV652.1 .W36 2023 (print) | LCC BV652.1 (ebook) | DDC 253—dc23/eng/20230420
LC record available at https://lccn.loc.gov/2023000835
LC ebook record available at https://lccn.loc.gov/2023000836

Published in association with the literary agency of WordServe Literary Group, Ltd., www.wordserveliterary.com.

Cover design: Faceout Studio, Spencer Fuller
Cover photos: © Mike Flippo, Roman Samokhin / Shutterstock
Interior design: Denise Froehlich

Printed in the United States of America

23 24 25 26 27   TRM   5 4 3 2 1

To my fellow kingdom laborers:
men and women, paid and volunteer, full time and part time,
those with public platforms and those toiling behind the scenes,
in the local church and in ministries across the globe.
Keep learning and keep leading.

CONTENTS

FOREWORD

I live every day with a great irony.

I write books and teach and speak on adaptive-change leadership. Adaptive change is the leadership approach for uncharted territory, for the moment when you realize that there isn't a map and you're going to have learn to navigate from the terrain itself.

For most leaders who have been trained to look for and identify best practices, adaptive leadership is awkward and even frustrating because it is what is utilized when there are no best practices. While technical problems can be solved by experts, adaptive challenges require shifts in perspective and behavior that will lead to learning. Technical problems are about applying what we know works; adaptive challenges begin in the moment when the leader does not know what to do but must lead on anyway.

Adaptive leadership requires experts to become learners—for those with a bent toward protecting their people to intentionally and carefully take them through loss, and to navigate competing values and creative experiments with a desire to discover what is new rather than master what has been familiar terrain. And mostly, adaptive leadership requires us to face the resistance of our own people, who are very likely beginning to lose trust in us even as they begin to take transformative steps.

So it makes sense that those who are being trained in this kind of leadership would want to know whether this approach actually works, even if we are not sure it will work this time, in this case, with this people, facing this challenge. You see, even though I teach adaptive leadership, what most people want from me is a technical solution. (Even having me come to speak or reading my books is often an unconscious attempt to find a technical solution for an adaptive problem.)

"Tod, can you give us an example of a group that made an adaptive change?" Every time I speak or teach about adaptive change, I get this question. Often it is the very first question asked. And behind it is a desire for an assurance that this hard but necessary way of leading people is worth it.

When asked, I often assure my questioner that yes, there are great examples. And no, I really am not going to share much of the detail with you. Why? Because human nature being what it is, you'll try to copy what the exemplars have done. Instead of learning how to lead adaptive change, you'll try to find a safe, quick fix that ensures that all will be well.

But even still, most of us benefit from hearing the stories of others—of at least learning what they learned and how they learned it. Like listening to an adventurer who survived a harrowing journey, we would love to glean some wisdom for when we venture out. We need not copy their plans but we want to learn from their instincts, analyze their decision-making, and test our own answers with those who have done this before.

Which is why Angie Ward's case-study approach is a gift.

Adaptive leadership thrives "from the balcony" (in Ronald Heifetz and Marty Linsky's memorable phrase). Adaptive leadership is best developed when leaders are able to get a larger perspective on the complex challenges that face them. Case studies like those in this book allow us to get on the balcony, look at someone else's challenges to see what we can learn, and even practice our own responses.

While the introduction to this book serves as a really fine primer on adaptive leadership, what is remarkable about this collection of case studies is the breadth of them. The range of topics reminds all of us that leadership is complicated, that humans are complicated, that the hardest decisions to make often begin in the fog of uncertainty and in the challenge of discernment.

This collection is also notable because these case studies are at the same time so common and so authentically complex. They are the kinds of issues that faith leaders face every day. But just because they are so recognizable doesn't mean they are easily resolved. Start reading any one of them and you'll quickly understand that what makes pastoral ministry so hard is the intricacy of detail and the inherent difficulty of discerning what to do when there are so many possible responses.

In one of my own books, I discuss at some length the reality that church leadership is like a family business. We have both relationships that are akin to a big extended family that are meant to be marked by unconditional love, and a mission to accomplish that requires goals, metrics, strategies, and budgets. As I wrote, "The organization that has inherently valuable relationships also has an instrumentally critical purpose." And navigating what are often constant "dual relationships" requires that pastors are both personal and professional, are both competent and compassionate, and both make hard decisions and demonstrate deep humility when facing the uncertainty of the unknown.

As I wrote then, "As a pastor, I knew that many people expected me to know everything there is to know about the mystery of God and every person's name in our congregation when I ran into them at the grocery store. We are expected to perfectly exegete and translate the Scriptures, and perfectly understand, translate and oversee the financials. Our board is both our customer and our client, and our partners and our bosses at the same time. Again, this is not to say that the Christian leader's work is harder than other leaders', but that the unique challenge of leadership includes managing emotional complexity amid all the demands."[1]

Navigating this demanding duality calls for the kind of practice that these case studies and the probing questions that accompany them offer.

We can all be grateful for it.

—TOD BOLSINGER
The DePree Center Church Leadership
Institute, Fuller Seminary
Author of *Canoeing the Mountain:
Leadership in Uncharted Territory*

---

1. Tod Bolsinger, *Canoeing the Mountains: Christian Leadership in Uncharted Territory* (Downers Grove, IL: InterVarsity Press, 2018), 232–33.

INTRODUCTION

Have you ever lost your GPS signal while navigating an unknown road?

A few years ago, I was driving home from a friend's musical performance at a small out-of-town theater in southern Indiana. There was a main, well-traveled route from the theater to my home in suburban Indianapolis, but it happened to be closed for construction. I had to take an unfamiliar, circuitous route that included a lot of narrow and winding roads, up and down backcountry hills. It was dusk, so between the setting sun and the shade of the overgrown trees lining the road, visibility was rapidly diminishing. As I made haste, my two passengers—a friend and her teenaged daughter—expressed some motion-induced discomfort, adding to my feelings of stress.

And then I lost my GPS signal.

Apparently my wireless provider's coverage did not extend to the southern hills of the Hoosier state. I had been in such a focused hurry to speed through the twists and turns, I hadn't noticed the signal bars disappearing one by one, until . . . nothing. No signal, no new instructions, and no idea where I was or where to go next.

It was not a good feeling.

After pausing to exhale and open the windows so we could

all take in some fresh air, I slowly continued driving. What else was I to do? We were in the middle of what felt like nowhere, and we couldn't call for help even if we wanted to. We all squinted to read road signs, trying to figure out the correct course. We did our best to avoid gravel roads, the woods, and the numerous lakes that dotted the area. Eventually—finally!—we returned to cell phone range and picked up a signal and directions to our destination. But my relieved chatter belied (or perhaps betrayed) my distress, because it took the rest of the evening for my nerves to settle and my stomach to unknot. And it was a few more days before I could calmly reflect on the experience, wondering whether I could have done anything differently.

I realized afterward that my predicament started with good planning but was thwarted by incorrect assumptions and unexpected circumstances. I knew the main road was closed and that I would need to take an alternate route. But I assumed I would have a wireless signal to maintain a connection to GPS navigation. When that failed, I didn't have a map or adequate lighting to see the roads and obstacles. I didn't know my passengers would develop motion sickness, and I wasn't prepared for my emotional response to their distress on top of my own feelings of frustration and panic.

This is very often what it feels like to navigate the complex challenges of real-life ministry leadership.

We may have a few maps, but they are likely outdated, incomplete, or unavailable. We know one main route, and that one is closed. Come to think of it, we may not even be sure exactly where we're headed. This is new territory, and the only thing we really know is that it's potentially treacherous. Every turn could reveal a new danger.

Meanwhile, we've got people on the journey with us, and

we feel the weight of responsibility for getting them safely to the destination. They're wondering what we're doing, where we're going, getting queasy from all the twists and turns, calling out suggestions in a cacophony that only adds to the disequilibrium we are experiencing.

It is not a good feeling to have to lead without a map. Yet at some point, every ministry leader will experience this challenge. Is it possible to prepare for it?

The Classroom Myth

A common observation by leaders when they experience real-life ministry is, "They didn't teach me this in Bible college/college/seminary!" That's because those environments generally are not supposed to. Most classes at the undergraduate and master's levels are designed to be foundational, providing preparation in basic theology, management, and ministry skills. Most students in these classes do not yet have an advanced experiential framework. It is only when they—we—get into real-life ministry and accumulate some experience and authority that we find we are not prepared for the integration required to address more complex leadership challenges.

Besides, even if a particular educational environment does incorporate a level of synthesis, there is simply no way to train for every specific scenario. At some point, we as leaders need to move beyond the basics and learn broader principles, along with how to integrate all that we have learned into complex, rapidly changing situations. And we need to learn to teach others these principles and integration. This really can happen only in real life, not in a classroom. And this type of leadership has a name: adaptive leadership.

An Introduction to Adaptive Leadership

Adaptive leadership theory was first described by Ronald Heifetz in his 1994 book, *Leadership without Easy Answers*. Unlike leadership theories that originate from the image of a leader influencing others from a distance on top or in front of an organization, adaptive leadership is uniquely follower focused. Heifetz defines adaptive leadership as "mobilizing people to tackle tough problems."[1] As Peter Northouse explains in his summative book about leadership theories, adaptive leadership "focuses primarily on how leaders help others do the work they need to do, in order to adapt to the challenges they face."[2]

Critical to an understanding of adaptive leadership theory is the differentiation between two types of leadership challenges: technical challenges and adaptive challenges.

Technical challenges are problems that are "clearly defined, with known solutions that can be implemented through existing organizational procedures."[3] For example, taking an organization through a facility expansion may stretch the leader's knowledge and capacity, but in general it is a technical challenge: the goal is clearly defined, and there are established best practices and a host of resources to help a leader manage the process, from vision casting to fundraising to construction.

Adaptive challenges, by contrast, are not clearly defined or easy to identify, and they cannot be solved by a leader's normal authority or expertise or with an organizational policy manual. In the case of the capital campaign, an adaptive challenge would

---

1. Ronald A. Heifetz, *Leadership without Easy Answers* (Cambridge, MA: Harvard Univ. Press, 1994), 15.
2. Peter G. Northouse, *Leadership: Theory and Practice*, 9th ed. (Newbury Park, CA: Sage Publishing, 2021), 258.
3. Ibid., 260.

arise if it were discovered that local residents were planning to challenge the project because they viewed the church as an unwelcoming, and unwelcome, neighbor.

Note that some problems may include both technical and adaptive challenges. The table outlines the three types of challenges a leader or an organization may encounter.

Problem	Solution	
	CLEAR/KNOWN	UNCLEAR/UNKNOWN
CLEAR/KNOWN	Technical	Combination
UNCLEAR/UNKNOWN		Adaptive

Three Types of Challenges: Technical, Adaptive, and a Combination of the Two

Adaptive leadership is about helping others learn how to navigate adaptive challenges, of which there are four primary types.[4]

The first is a *gap between espoused values and behavior*. A person, group, or organization may state a particular belief or value, but their actions do not match this stated belief. For example, I once served at a church where a stated value was that staff members must demonstrate both "proven character and proven ministry." One of the music ministers was widely known as narcissistic and emotionally abusive, but because of his musical gifts and the quality of the Sunday program, his character issues went unaddressed.

The second type of adaptive challenge exists when there are *competing commitments* within a group or organization. For example, commitments to honesty and truth-telling might compete with commitments to privacy and confidentiality. Or one party within an organization may value one thing while another

---

4. Ibid., 264.

values something else, such as when a financial committee is dedicated to not taking on additional debt while another committee seeks a facility expansion. As you can see, often the conflict can be between two equally important and valid commitments.

The third type of adaptive challenge is that of *speaking the unspeakable*. For whatever reason, there is a resistance to naming the situation. As Northouse explains, "The phrases 'sacred cow' and 'elephant in the room' are examples of this archetype; it occurs when there are radical ideas, unpopular issues, or conflicting perspectives that people don't address because of their sensitive or controversial nature. Speaking out about these is seen as 'risky.'"[5] For example, no one may want to acknowledge a beloved pastor's failing health and the possibilities of forced retirement or planned succession.

The fourth primary type of adaptive challenge is *work avoidance*. This occurs when people use diversionary tactics to avoid dealing with challenging issues. In ministry, I have seen leaders put off hard but necessary conversations in the name of "being loving" or because "the timing wasn't right," even though the issue was clearly having a negative impact on the organization.

Remember that adaptive leadership is about helping others navigate adaptive challenges, and that navigating adaptive challenges "usually require[s] changes in people's priorities, beliefs, roles, and values."[6] Because these priorities, beliefs, and values are always deeply rooted and deeply held, acting in a manner contrary to them may be unthinkable to some. Challenging them, therefore, elicits a host of emotional reactions.

Richard R. Dunn explains:

---

5. Ibid.
6. Ibid., 262.

Adaptive challenge can always be traced to a disruptive force, internally or externally, that signals the end of a season of stability and status quo. The greater the disruptive force, the greater the demand for and scope of adaptive change. When there are multiple disruptive forces in play, both internally and externally, the process of adaptive change will likely be experienced as a crisis. For those stakeholders whose success is most closely tied to the past season of stability and status quo, the crisis will be perceived as a threat. For those whose success appears most closely tied to a reimagined future, the crisis will be embraced as an opportunity.[7]

Foundational to adaptive leadership theory is a systems perspective: the notion that problems are complex, always changing, and connected to each other.[8] Because of this interconnection, within a system "every change changes everything." But this potential volatility also drives systems to seek equilibrium and stability. Therefore, human systems will work very hard to regain balance. I'm sure we can all give plenty of examples of congregational and staff meetings where we have seen these systemic realities play out. Sworn adversaries become best friends and allies in the face of a new common enemy. Congregants blame anyone else—often and especially the pastor—in an attempt to offload responsibility for their own actions and emotions. Leaders become defensive or they double down and become more demanding, spreading their anxiety to everyone else. Parties claim moral or spiritual high ground to discredit their opponents. The communications "grapevine" grows and spreads, choking healthy conflict and conversation in the process.

---

7. Richard R. Dunn, author's personal correspondence.
8. Northouse, *Leadership*, 258.

The practice of adaptive leadership is clearly not for the faint of heart. As Heifetz writes, "In adaptive situations, fulfilling the social functions of authority requires walking a razor's edge. Challenge people too fast, and they will push the authority figure over to failing their expectations of stability. But challenge people too slowly, and they will throw him [sic] down when they discover that no progress has been made. . . . In either case, an authority figure cuts his feet."[9]

And yet, leaders have a responsibility to help others through these difficult spaces—to build mature disciples through the down-and-dirty, even dangerous work of adaptive leadership. As Tod Bolsinger describes it, "Leadership is energizing a community of people toward their own transformation in order to accomplish a shared mission in the face of a changing world."[10] This powerful potential is what makes adaptive leadership well worth the work.

The Behaviors of Adaptive Leaders

So what does adaptive leadership look like? It will take shape differently depending on our personalities, relationships, and communication styles, but adaptive leadership involves six key behaviors:[11]

1. *Get on the balcony.* It can be easy for leaders to lose sight of the big picture because we have gotten caught up in the action on the ground. But adaptive leadership requires a mix of action and reflection, much like the difference

9. Heifetz, *Leadership without Easy Answers*, 126.
10. Tod Bolsinger, *Canoeing the Mountains: Christian Leadership in Uncharted Territory* (Downers Grove, IL: InterVarsity Press, 2015), 36.
11. Northouse, *Leadership*, 290.

between being part of a dance versus watching the patterns on the dance floor from a higher perch.[12] An effective adaptive leader will be able to move back and forth between these views.

2. *Identify adaptive challenges.* From the balcony, a leader must correctly identify the challenges at hand, including whether they are technical or adaptive, because each type requires a different response. Many times leadership failure can be attributed to misdiagnosis of the problem. Since adaptive challenges cause emotional distress, examining this distress can often give clues regarding the nature of the problem. However, adaptive challenges will sometimes present as conflict over technical issues such as structures, procedures, schedules, authority, or aesthetics.[13] According to Heifetz, the key question for differentiating between technical and adaptive challenges is, "Does making progress on this problem require changes in people's values, attitudes, habits or behavior?" If so, it is most likely an adaptive challenge.

3. *Regulate distress.* Northouse uses the term "protection" to describe the leader's role in managing the rate of adaptive change,[14] while Heifetz refers to pacing.[15] This is the challenging art at the heart of adaptive leadership: determining how much pressure to apply or discomfort to allow, where and in what amount, so that the challenge and the accompanying change do not overwhelm the system. Heifetz uses the helpful visual of a pressure cooker: "Keep the heat up without blowing up

12. Heifetz, *Leadership without Easy Answers*, 252.
13. Ibid., 254.
14. Northouse, *Leadership*, 260.
15. Heifetz, *Leadership without Easy Answers*, 39.

the vessel."[16] A good adaptive leader will navigate this tension and make changes as needed to keep situations within an acceptable range of distress.

4. *Maintain disciplined attention.* Because people do not like the feeling of disequilibrium brought about by the prospect or process of change, they will go to almost any length to avoid it. As Northouse explains, "this avoidance behavior can take many forms. People can ignore the problem on the authority, blame coworkers for the problem, attack those who want to address the problem, pretend the problem does not exist, or work hard in areas unrelated to the problem."[17] In the midst of this, the adaptive leader needs to keep people's attention focused on the real issues, not perceived problems that in reality are just distractions.

5. *Give the work back to the people.* Remember that navigating adaptive challenges involves changes in people's attitudes, values, habits, or behaviors. Therefore, the problem-solving also needs to take place in the hearts and minds of the people.[18] This is another way adaptive leadership is critically different from technical leadership. When faced with a technical challenge, a leader usually has the expertise and authority to define and solve the problem on their own. With an adaptive challenge, however, a leader must encourage, equip, and allow followers to manage the challenge at an appropriate pace. Even this is an artful dance of knowing how much followers can handle on their own and how much a leader must step in to provide direction.

---

16. Ibid., 128.
17. Northouse, *Leadership*, 268.
18. Heifetz, *Leadership without Easy Answers*, 121.

6. *Protect leadership voices from below.* This behavior involves listening "to the ideas of people who may be at the fringe, marginalized, or even deviant within the group or organization."[19] As Northouse points out, this is difficult and upsetting because it is disruptive to the status quo. Nevertheless, "Adaptive leaders should try to resist the tendency to minimize or shut down minority voices for the sake of the majority."[20] Doing so empowers all the members of the system, resulting in greater engagement and higher group morale.

The ultimate goal of ongoing adaptive leadership is not just to mobilize a group of people to tackle one tough problem. It is to help them develop "adaptive capacity," an ongoing and increasing ability to clarify values and to respond to challenges related to those values. The result is healthier organizations and systems that can flourish regardless of the circumstances.

COVID-19: A Global Adaptive Challenge

The COVID-19 pandemic was (and in many ways, continues to be) a textbook adaptive challenge on a global scale. From our personal lives to our professional work to our families and faith communities, COVID-19 brought a myriad of challenges without easy solutions: Should children go to school with masks, or should they be kept at home? How should churches respond to constantly changing guidelines about corporate gatherings? Should we travel to our relative's wedding across the country,

---

19. Northouse, *Leadership*, 270.
20. Ibid.

and should we bring our elderly grandmother? And before considering solutions, are we even clear about the problems?

Dilemmas like these raised questions that tapped into and sometimes challenged deep-seated beliefs and values. For example:

- What constitutes and contributes to the health of an individual, a community, a society, an economy?[21]
- Are mandates—of social distancing, of masks, of quarantines, of vaccines—a violation of individual liberty, or an exercise of civic or perhaps even Christian responsibility?
- Who gets to define the terms and decide who is right? Is jurisdiction individual, communal, regional, or national?

The ongoing effects of the pandemic have been joined by the usual adaptive challenges in our ministries: the stuff that we can't predict and that we can't learn in school. That is why now more than ever, it is critical for us to learn and practice the skills of adaptive leadership, helping those in our spheres of influence to develop the capacity to adjust and spread the love of Jesus in a VUCA—volatile, uncertain, complex, and ambiguous—world.[22]

Learning via Case Studies

Before my husband and I had children—and then as we moved through their stages of development and the accompanying parenting challenges—we watched families ahead of us on the

---

21. For more about these issues, see Angie Ward, *When the Universe Cracks: Living as God's People in Times of Crisis* (Colorado Springs, CO: NavPress, 2021).
22. Jeroen Kraaijenbrink, "What Does VUCA Really Mean?" *Forbes*, December 19, 2018, www.forbes.com/sites/jeroenkraaijenbrink/2018/12/19/what-does-vuca-really -mean/?sh=66678b817d62.

journey, wanting to learn from their experiences, both positive and negative. In the car on the way home from a social gathering, we'd talk about what we had witnessed: "What did you like or not like about how those parents responded? How would *we* have handled that situation? What are the principles and values that might guide our decisions?" In effect, we were learning via the *case study method,* observing and discussing real-world situations to clarify our values and potential responses in similar situations down the road.

The case study method was developed as a teaching tool by Harvard Business School nearly a century ago. By studying and discussing actual situations, leaders learn to identify important information, consider options, and propose solutions to complex problems. "Lectures can teach you *what* to think but now *how* to think," notes author William Ellet.[23] "To practice using knowledge in actual situations, you need some way of immersing yourself in both the available facts and the fluidity and uncertainty that characterize the real world. That's what cases are for."[24]

Ellet points out that most cases center around one of three main issues:

- "The need to make a critical *decision* and potentially persuade other characters in the case to accept it.
- "The need to perform an in-depth *evaluation* that lays out the pros and cons or strengths and weaknesses of the subject of the case.
- "The need to perform a comprehensive *problem diagnosis*

---

23. William C. Ellet, *The Case Study Handbook: How to Read, Discuss, and Write Persuasively about Cases* (Cambridge, MA: Harvard Business Review Press, 2007), 9.
24. Ibid., 14.

that identifies the root causes of a problem described in the case."[25]

Furthermore, cases are often nonlinear, can contain conflicting information and distracting details, and have no clear right answer—what Ellet calls "organized disorganization."[26] In other words, they describe adaptive challenges.

There are few books that center leadership learning in real-life case studies. There are even fewer that do this with application to ministry contexts. *Uncharted Leadership* incorporates the best of the leadership literature along with biblical and theological principles and perspectives into the practice of adaptive leadership.

Navigating This Book

This book uses case studies to explore and develop the practice of adaptive leadership in ministry. The cases contained within these pages are not quite "ripped from the headlines," but they describe actual situations encountered by actual ministry leaders. They have been gleaned from my experience and from friends, colleagues, and students. While the cases are unique, the underlying issues represent common challenges for all ministry leaders:

- Trust
- Communication
- Power
- Systems dynamics
- Conflict management

---

25. Ibid., 19.
26. Ibid., 17.

- Decision-making
- Team-building
- Organizational change

Some of the cases involve only the leadership of the organization, and the congregation has no idea what is going on. Others are public situations within a congregation, perhaps extending beyond to the community, even to the point of becoming (or potentially becoming) national news. They are drawn from all types of ministry contexts: churches and parachurch and educational organizations of various sizes and ages, representing a variety of locations, denominations, traditions, structures, and systems. In each case, names have been changed to protect real identities.

Each chapter starts with the description of the situation. The amount of information provided varies: some cases contain more details than others. In addition, some of the cases are presented using a more sequential writing structure, while others require you to do more work to piece together the details and see the big picture. In this book as in real life, cases are often told from one perspective, so you may also have to consider what the unnamed perspectives might be.

Following the details of the case, you will find a list of questions for consideration and discussion. Some of these questions are standard to every chapter—What other information do you wish you had? What are the issues involved? What are the risks and opportunities here?—while some questions explore nuances of the particular case. For example, would the challenges, and the adaptive leadership skills required, be different if some of the details of the case were changed? Remember, in a system, every change changes everything, so a change to one detail or decision can change the nature and trajectory of an entire situation.

In addition to questions about case information, this section includes questions to guide readers toward values clarification, including exploration of the biblical and theological principles that might shape those values. For example, What is the role of the pastor? What does it mean to restore someone who has fallen into sin? How might a leader protect the vulnerable in his or her care?

The discussion questions are followed by a commentary section in which I point out some of the critical issues, biblical and theological concerns, and possible outcomes of the case. Next, I provide some additional questions, now that the case and its key issues are becoming clearer from the information you have received. These include questions about your own assumptions and experiences and how they might be influencing your interpretation and diagnosis of the case.

I then provide an epilogue with any information known about how the case played out in real life, to satisfy your curiosity and to see the consequences, positive and negative, short and long term, of leadership decisions. Some have neat and clean endings; most do not. From there, I add a few "postmortem" reflection questions now that you know how the case ended, as well as several questions for your own application. How can you and your organization learn and grow from this case? What preemptive actions can you take to prepare for a situation like this in your ministry?

Each chapter concludes with a list of recommended resources for digging deeper into the topics pertaining to the case. Please note that inclusion of a book does not necessarily imply my wholesale endorsement. Rather, I have attempted to provide a sampling of resources to help you explore the issues in a case. Frankly, some of the cases are so complex or unique that it was difficult to find resources that address the issues involved. In addition, most of the resources are books; while there are excellent materials to be found online, these can change or be deleted. The resources suggested were accurate and available as of this writing.

The back of the book contains a bibliography with even more resources, followed by an index that lists all cases by topic. I hope you'll read all of the cases in this book, but if you are looking for cases about specific issues—say, for example, mental illness—you'll find a list of the relevant case titles in this index.

This book can be used in a number of ways: for individual reading and growth; in a formal classroom as a primary or supplemental course text and facilitated by an instructor; by ministry leadership teams to help discover and embed values; or for discussion with a mastermind or leadership peer group. No matter how you use this book, it's designed for you and your conversation partners to ask yourself, What would I/we do in this situation?

As you read the cases, I encourage you to engage with them honestly and seriously. You definitely won't identify with every detail of every case. Don't dismiss any of them just because you don't agree with or relate to parts of them such as theological bent, the details pertaining to the characters, or the type of organization, structure, or context. Instead, truly imagine yourself in the situation. Look for the commonalities that you and your ministry may share with the personalities, emotions, and underlying issues presented in each story. Reflect theologically without spiritualizing or moralizing your perspective. And don't wave a magic wand or suggest easy solutions that wouldn't reflect reality, like using your charming mediator skills to hold a meeting and get everyone on the same page in just an hour. The more you interact with these scenarios in deep, realistic ways, the more you'll get out of them.

While this book cannot serve as a map for every leadership challenge you may experience down the road, my hope is that by working through the case studies and questions presented in this book, you will develop compass points—in the form of clarified values and deeper conceptual understanding—that will better equip you to navigate the terrain in your particular leadership context.

Let's hit the trail.

01 | OVER THE HILLSIDE

D. J. Marino wearily climbed into his SUV and dialed his wife.

"How'd it go?" she asked cautiously as she checked the clock. By her calculations, the meeting had gone on for nearly three hours.

"It was the worst I've ever seen," D. J. said. "Our worship leader ran out of the building crying and probably isn't coming back. We almost disfellowshiped a member from the floor during the meeting. And I almost quit in the middle of it." His wife groaned.

D. J. ended the call and pointed his car toward home. He was exhausted. Less than a month earlier, Hillside Christian Church held what he felt was an energy-filled Easter celebration. Now the church seemed to be falling apart before his eyes. In more than twenty-five years of pastoral ministry, D. J. had seen a lot, but never anything like this.

The previous fall, D. J. had accepted a call to become interim pastor at Hillside Christian Church. Hillside was located in a small country community twenty-five minutes from a major city. D. J.'s predecessor, Timothy Reed, had served the church for thirty-three years before retiring during the COVID-19 pandemic. While attendance had declined during the pandemic and from the church's heyday, Hillside seemed to have a solid core of about seventy-five committed attendees and leaders, many of whom were related to one another and had been with the church for decades. During the search process, everyone agreed that the church needed some fresh energy. D. J. arrived ready to love and lead Hillside via his usual combination of pastoral care and solid preaching.

The first few months were generally encouraging. Thanks to D. J.'s strong preaching and outgoing personality, the Sunday worship services reflected a noticeable bump in energy when he arrived, which many noted with gratitude. The elders and deacons councils were eager to seek D. J.'s counsel on leadership issues. D. J. and his wife received numerous invitations to join church members for meals and other social events.

It wasn't until a few months into the new year that D. J. noticed a small cloud on the horizon. The church, in consultation with its denominational overseer, had begun the search for a new senior pastor. During discussions about compensation, the search team brought up the matter of housing. Hillside's property included a parsonage, but years ago Timothy had moved out and purchased a private residence in the community. The church then decided to rent the parsonage to Mark and Sue Kingston, a young couple in the church.

Nearly ten years later, the parsonage was still occupied by the Kingstons, who had since added several children to their family. The family rented the house at a significant discount compared with market price because the church did not need the parsonage and the family had some financial challenges.

In addition, during this time Sue Kingston's father, Ed, had been voted an elder at Hillside. When no one else seemed available or interested, Ed had accepted the role and had served dutifully and, it appeared to D. J., selflessly for the last several years, eventually becoming chair of the board of elders. Ed's wife, meanwhile, had been appointed to the pastoral search team. Such was the nature and need at Hillside: as a small congregation, individuals, their spouses, and immediate family members often filled multiple leadership roles. As another example, the volunteer worship leader also served on the pastoral search team, while his wife ran the sound board during Sunday services.

The search team did not want to evict the Kingstons from the parsonage because of their financial need and because they were not sure how Ed and his wife would respond. They decided not to include the parsonage housing as part of the compensation package for the next long-term pastor. However, it was pointed out that the suggested salary—for what would likely be a three-quarters' time pastoral position—would probably not allow the pastor to live in or near the community, because home values in the area had risen exponentially over the last decade.

As the search team considered the parsonage issue and worked with the district overseer to finalize a job description and post the position, D. J. oversaw the planning for the upcoming Easter Sunday celebration, which would include a number of beloved church traditions. The spirit at Hillside seemed positive and hopeful. Volunteer leaders had new energy and continued to respond favorably to D. J.'s encouragement. Easter Sunday itself seemed to reflect the congregation's mood, as a bright sun welcomed joyful celebrants to a pancake breakfast, egg hunt, and worship celebration.

D. J. gave an enthusiastic report to family and friends who gathered at his house for dinner later that afternoon. The service had drawn Hillside's largest crowd since the start of the pandemic more than a year ago. He noted the storm cloud of the unresolved parsonage issue but was encouraged by the spirit he had experienced among the congregation that morning.

Then D. J. got a phone call from Reggie Holt.

Reggie was a relatively new member of the board of deacons and a member of the search team. D. J. had not interacted with him much to this point, but during their first interaction it quickly became clear that Reggie had some very strong opinions about the search, the church, and his fellow leaders.

Reggie began calling D. J. regularly to weigh in on the matters at hand. He believed the church was operating illegally in regard to the parsonage, and sent D. J. articles and state legal codes regarding improper benefits for board members of not-for-profit organizations. He accused Ed of becoming an elder so that his daughter could live in the parsonage. Reggie also said the search team had been talking about Ed behind his back.

Reggie wasn't the only one bending D. J.'s ear. As word got out via the small-church grapevine about the parsonage issue, other members began calling, texting, and emailing D. J. to give their perspectives about Hillside's problems. According to these congregants, there were a lot of problems, they had been unresolved for years, and it was everyone else's fault. Rumors, accusations, and misinformation began to run rampant: about other congregants, about the parsonage, about the previous pastor, even about the denomination.

D. J. spent hours upon hours listening, questioning, exhorting, placating. His fitness watch calculated thousands of steps as he paced his house, trying to reason over the phone with agitated congregants. For six months, the church brimmed with potential. Now it seemed Hillside was overflowing with poison. D. J. found deep-seated mistrust everywhere he looked. Longtime families were leaving.

"It's like Pastor Timothy had been the dad at the family dinner table for thirty-three years," D. J. lamented to an old seminary classmate over lunch one day. "When Dad was at the table, everyone else knew how to act. But when he retired, everyone looked around, realized Dad was gone, and started a huge food fight."

Growing increasingly exasperated, D. J. at one point chided the congregation at its quarterly business meeting. He had just preached that morning from Ephesians about the unity of the church. "This is when we need to pull together, and instead you are tearing yourselves apart!" he admonished. Later, at the same meeting, Reggie shouted at the worship leader's wife, causing the worship leader to run out of the room. In response, someone came up to D. J. and asked if they could immediately vote to disfellowship Reggie from the floor. Feeling his frustration getting the better of him, D. J. recused himself from the meeting and to his office to regain his composure.

QUESTIONS FOR REFLECTION

1. With the information you've been given, how would you summarize the problem(s) in this case?

2. Who are the main characters and what are their roles in this situation?

3. What assumptions and values do you hear voiced by these characters?

4. What other information do you wish you had about this situation?

5. What seem to be the technical challenges involved in this case?

6. What are the adaptive challenges, and what type of adaptive challenges are they?

7. What risks and opportunities do you see in this case?

8. What biblical and theological principles should be considered in this case?

9. What are your suggested next steps for the parties involved?

10. What longer-term considerations might impact short-term decisions?

11. What work should be given "back to the people" here? To whom, and how?

12. What assumptions and values guide your recommended course of action?

13. What responses did you notice within yourself as you read this case?

14. Do you think anything could have been done differently, either individually or organizationally, to avoid this situation? If so, what?

15. Might this case be different if:

    a) Hillside Christian Church were larger?

    b) The church were located in a large city instead of a small community?

    c) D. J. were the permanent pastor, not an interim?

16. Issues to consider:

    a) What is the role of a church's constitution and bylaws?

Are there ever extenuating circumstances when an organization's constitution or bylaws should not be followed? If so, what might be examples?

b) What is the responsibility of a church to offer a realistic living wage for the area in which it is located?

c) What should be the limits regarding members holding multiple roles in the church?

d) What can a leader do if conflicting parties are not willing to work toward a solution?

e) Is there ever a time when the perceived needs of an organization override the law?

Commentary

D. J. has inherited more than he bargained for. During his thirty-three-year tenure, Pastor Timothy established patterns of leadership and relationship that seem to have resulted in a deep, unresolved well of conflict. For many years, there was no need to address the parsonage issue or other conflict. Everything just worked, and everyone played nice with each other for Pastor Timothy. But in the wake of his departure, some individuals sensed an opportunity to voice their agendas and seek a measure of control over the future of the church. This caused the hidden conflict to surface and exposed widely divergent perspectives about the role of leadership, the process of church governance, how to handle conflict, and the nature and sources of the problems at hand.

While Hillside appeared to have a small but healthy core of congregants, the church was really held together by a few longtime, superinvolved extended families. Mistrust had been eroding those relationships for years; when the conflict erupted, the departure of those families depleted almost all of the church's leadership and volunteer ranks. Without willingness by any of those parties to accept responsibility for their actions or to seek reconciliation, D. J. and the church face a steep, perhaps insurmountable, climb.

| ADDITIONAL QUESTIONS |

1. Has your initial diagnosis of this situation changed? If so, how and why?

2. Which character(s) do you find yourself empathizing with?

3. Do you need to revise or address any of your assumptions?

Epilogue

As more congregants and leaders departed and the depth of the mistrust was revealed, D. J. realized that Hillside might not be left with the critical mass of people needed to support a new pastor. He suggested as much to the denominational overseer, who reluctantly agreed and began exploring options via his network, including a merger with a congregation in a nearby town and a relaunch of Hillside with several prospective church planters. However, none of these options panned out.

Meanwhile, D. J. and the overseer scheduled a congregational meeting with a trained conflict-mediation specialist. That meeting was the church's biggest gathering since Easter Sunday, and a number of departed members returned, ready to air their grievances. However, the mediator encouraged individuals toward private reconciliation, and several more families soon announced their departure.

D. J. valiantly attempted to hold things together. He became the worship leader when the previous leader never came back after the contentious quarterly meeting. He pushed factious parties to talk to one another and to work toward reconciliation. He tried to encourage the remaining leaders, including Ed and his wife, who were discouraged and exhausted. "I feel like a carpet that's been hung over a clothesline and repeatedly beaten," Ed told D. J.

Finally, over lunch with the two remaining elders, D. J. voiced the question it seemed no one wanted to ask.

"It sounds like you guys want to know how much longer you have to keep this going," he said. The two men nodded.

From there, the demise was swift. In consultation with the denominational overseer, D. J. and the remaining elders agreed that the church was now on life support, and they were too weary to keep up the fight. Following Hillside's constitution and bylaws, the congregation received notice that a meeting would be held in two weeks to determine the future of the church. Reggie and others, many of whom had left the church but communicated to the congregation via mass emails, continued to blame current leadership, calling for everyone to step down.

Four months after the joyful Easter service, the membership—or what was left of it—voted to close the church. D. J. called for the vote after several hours of finger-pointing by a disgruntled few who positioned themselves as martyrs for trying to save the church. While approximately twenty members had been in attendance at the start of the meeting, the final vote was twelve to two, including three absentee votes, because a handful of congregants had walked out before the vote was taken.

The decision took effect immediately. After seventy-two

years as a light in the community, Hillside Christian Church was closed. Several members lingered after the meeting ended, sitting or sobbing in silence. D. J. did his best to console them, thanking those who had served the church faithfully for generations.

On his way out of the building as he carried personal effects from his office to his car, D. J. came upon Reggie delivering an animated diatribe toward Ed. D. J. couldn't believe it. "Really?" he asked Reggie, shaking his head.

D. J. got into his SUV and turned out of the parking lot of Hillside Christian Church one last time, pausing momentarily to text his wife:

"It's over."

NOW WHAT?

1. How do you feel now that you've read the entire case and know how it ended?

2. Would you have acted similarly?

3. How could a different result have been achieved?

4. What actions can you, your fellow leaders, and your organization take to prepare for—and perhaps avoid, mitigate, or replicate—this particular situation or outcome?

Recommended Resources

Hammar, Richard R. *Church Governance: What Leaders Must Know to Conduct Legally Sound Church Business.* Carol Stream, IL: Christianity Today International, 2019.

Herrington, Jim, Mike Bonem, and James H. Furr. *Leading Congregational Change: A Practical Guide for the Transformational Journey*. Minneapolis: Fortress, 2000.

Vaters, Karl. *Small Church Essentials: Field-Tested Principles for Leading a Healthy Congregation of under 250*. Chicago: Moody, 2018.

Woolverton, David E. *Mission Rift: Leading through Church Conflict*. Minneapolis: Fortress, 2021.

02 | GROWING PAINS

Providence Church was a ten-year-old, nondenominational, multisite church in ten congregations across one state. Formed by the merger of two churches, one nearly fifty years old and one approximately ten years old, Providence experienced rapid growth in its first decade. The size of its ten congregations varied, from 125 attendees at the smallest to more than 2,500 at the largest, for a total of more than 10,000 attendees across all sites. While most of the congregations were located throughout the state's ethnically diverse major metropolitan area, several were situated at the far north and south ends of the state, about four hours from each other and two hours from the central city, but even farther apart from the city demographically and politically.

Providence Church was distinct from many multisite churches in that each congregation had its own elders and live preaching. Each congregation had one lead pastor while the overall church had a charismatic senior pastor, Oscar Beckett, responsible for shepherding the overall church, its ten congregations, and their ten pastors. Oscar's father-in-law had been the founder of the larger of the two merged churches and the architect of the merger, eventually passing the leadership mantle to Oscar and other leaders.

The ten lead pastors of the congregations formed a lead team, which met regularly to guide the church. Additionally, the preaching pastors gathered for a team meeting ten days in advance of each sermon, during which the preaching pastors shared thoughts and notes on the same passage to be preached in each congregation. The church had set up a centralized budget and human resources department, and pooled funding to benefit all ten congregations. The goal of this structure was to enable the congregations to be gospel centered and outward focused, with a desire to be contextualized yet unified. The model also facilitated shared resources for church planting in under-resourced areas.

The COVID-19 era challenged this mode of governance as the responses to various issues such as masks, lockdowns, vaccines, and racial justice tended to be contextualized and varied according to each congregation, depending on their location in or outside of the city. As a result, it became more difficult to be unified in an approach to these issues.

A further possibility for conflict arose at the formation of an executive team consisting of just four of the lead pastors. The stated rationale was that a ten-member team was too large for effective decision-making. The smaller executive team provided more centralized and agile leadership, which was especially helpful during the pandemic. However, the change in structure caused conflict with some of the lead pastors. Those who were not included in the shift began to lose trust in the church's leadership as a whole and believed their voices had been diminished. Two stories emerged about how the change in structure came about: one was that the leadership team voted to go in this direction, while the other was that the leadership team was merely informed by Oscar that the change had been made.

No matter which story was accurate, the result was that in just a little more than a year, four lead pastors either resigned or were removed—again, depending on perspective—from their positions. Each of the lead pastors had unique reasons for their transitions, including conflict with the real or perceived understanding of church trajectory and vision; dispute over how a specific congregation related to the whole; personal marital struggle; and a desire to do more in the areas of social justice and racial unrest. Between the pandemic and the leadership changes, the church lost many attenders and experienced a sharp decline in giving. Trust in leadership was at an all-time low, both at the congregational level and among the leadership team.

At this point, Oscar took an extended sabbatical, speaking of a desire to recover from the significant amount of pain and grief over losses he and others had faced in the preceding year.

QUESTIONS FOR REFLECTION

1. With the information you've been given, how would you summarize the problem(s) in this case?

2. Who are the main characters and what are their roles in this situation?

3. What assumptions and values do you hear voiced by these characters?

4. What other information do you wish you had about this situation?

5. What seem to be the technical challenges involved in this case?

6. What are the adaptive challenges, and what type of adaptive challenges are they?

7. What risks and opportunities do you see in this case?

8. What biblical and theological principles should be considered in this case?

9. What are your suggested next steps for the parties involved?

10. What longer-term considerations might impact short-term decisions?

11. What work should be given "back to the people" here? To whom, and how?

12. What assumptions and values guide your recommended course of action?

13. What responses did you notice within yourself as you read this case?

14. Do you think anything could have been done differently, either individually or organizationally, to avoid this situation? If so, what?

15. Might this case be different if:

    a) All of the churches in the network were located in similar cultural, ethnic, and sociopolitical contexts?

    b) The churches were more similar to each other in size?

    c) Oscar were not the son-in-law of one of the founding pastors?

    d) The churches were more spread out, so that none were within driving distance of another?

16. Issues to consider:

   a) In any type of multicongregational system, where is the balance between autonomy and unity? What are the potential strengths and weaknesses of moving to either end of the spectrum?

   b) Why and how must leadership structures change as an organization grows? How do you know when the structure needs to change? What principles and practices should guide the creation or change of these structures?

   c) What facilitates or hinders trust in an organization's leadership? What can be done to regain trust when it has eroded?

Commentary

Providence Church's desire to be contextual yet unified among its congregations is admirable. However, as the church has grown, it seems these values have come into increasing tension with one another. The contextual differences have become a source of division rather than a strength for building up the church and sharing the gospel in different settings. The rapid growth of the church has outpaced its leadership structure. Attempts to change them have led to a loss in trust, staff, attendance, and giving, further complicating the church's post-COVID recovery. Can Providence grow in size while retaining both church unity and contextual diversity, or are these values too at odds with one another?

But the growing pains are not only organizational. Oscar must now continue to grow in his ability to lead beyond his charismatic personality, raw gifts, and inherited authority, and to develop his skills as the leader of an increasingly complex ministry organization. Providence's growth in size, maturity, and efficacy is inextricably linked to Oscar's growth as a leader.

| ADDITIONAL QUESTIONS |

- Has your initial diagnosis of this situation changed? If so, how and why?

- Which character(s) do you find yourself empathizing with?

- Do you need to revise or address any of your assumptions?

Epilogue

Oscar came back from his sabbatical a revitalized man. Whereas it seemed he had been "in hiding" for the two years prior to his break, he returned much more present and proximate. Even though Providence had more than four hundred employees, Oscar invited anyone to reach out to him with any concerns. By all accounts, he was a careful listener to anyone who responded to this invitation.

Meanwhile, Providence's leadership team realized that the real issue was not politics or differing positions on social justice, women's issues, or medical issues, because all of these would continue beyond a pandemic and election cycles. Instead, the real issue was clarity around power, roles, process, and strategy, and the trust engendered by this clarity. What seemed to be the presenting issues were just amplifiers of the real issues.

Providence needed a new governance approach that would allow for centralized leadership to flourish, even as the contextual leaders were able to shepherd faithfully. To that end, the leadership team decided to invite two more individuals to join the executive team. This time, however, rather than pulling from the lead-pastor team, the two additions were non-lead pastors from within the Providence family of churches. Furthermore, these two men were in their midsixties, bringing much-needed wisdom and leadership experience to a team primarily of younger pastors. The decision-making process was also clarified, with decisions now made by an executive team but approved by vote of the larger leadership team.

In addition, some of the executive team began meeting with the diverse congregations to just sit together, be a sounding board, and listen to updates and concerns. This new emphasis of getting leadership, staff, and congregants together around a meal, what Providence began to call "tabling," greatly helped in rebuilding communication and trust at all levels within the organization. Pastors from all congregations reported feeling rejuvenated, energized, and hopeful for the future of Providence Church. Attendance and giving also picked back up. While challenges lie ahead as the church begins to grow again, it appears that Providence will be well positioned to face those challenges.

Now What?

1. How do you feel now that you've read the entire case and know how it ended?

2. Would you have acted similarly?

3. How could a different result have been achieved?

4. What actions can you, your fellow leaders, and your organization take to prepare for—and perhaps avoid, mitigate, or replicate—this particular situation or outcome?

Recommended Resources

Anderson, Robert J., and William A. Adams. *Scaling Leadership: Building Organizational Capability and Capacity to Create Outcomes That Matter Most.* Hoboken, NJ: Wiley, 2019.

House, Brad, and Gregg Allison. *MultiChurch: Exploring the Future of Multisite.* Grand Rapids: Zondervan, 2017.

Quinn, Robert E. *Deep Change: Discovering the Leader Within.* San Francisco: Jossey-Bass, 1996.

CHAPTER

03 | SUCCESSION STORY

Camp JOY (Jesus, Others, and You) is a Christian camp in the upper Midwest. Camp JOY was founded in the mid-1950s by a young pastor, Howard Thornton, who had been commissioned as a missionary by a children's evangelism ministry that had been founded a decade earlier. Howard moved to the north woods along with his wife, their four children, and Howard's sister and brother-in-law, Dorothy and Walter Larson, who had been recruited by Howard to join them in this new venture.

Over the years, Camp JOY enjoyed steady growth, to the point that forty years later, the camp served seven thousand people per year through a variety of year-round programs, including summer children's camps, youth adventure trips, family camps, and weekend retreat groups. Under Howard as general director, the camp was run by a full-time "missionary staff" of twenty men and women, all of whom raised their own financial support to work at Camp JOY. In addition to Howard's brother-in-law, Walter Larson, the staff included two of Howard's adult sons, Brian and Dennis. Brian served as operations director, while Dennis served as program director. Howard reported to a board of directors who met at the camp three times a year.

As Howard approached his seventieth birthday, he announced his retirement to the board. Realizing the importance of a full search to replace the camp's founder, the board appointed one of its own members, Anthony Walker, to serve as interim director. Anthony lived in a large city six hours away, but his full-time job allowed him to travel to Camp JOY regularly during his interim appointment to check in with staff and make major decisions. During his absences, the tight-knit, longtime staff kept operations going as usual under the leadership of Brian and Dennis Thornton.

As the board began a full search for a new general director, Howard expressed his desire that one of his sons be selected to take the reins. Indeed, both Brian and Dennis interviewed for the position, but the board ended up selecting an outside candidate, Rick Schneider. Rick came to Camp JOY with a seminary degree and effective leadership experience at several major camps and retreat centers around the US. The board felt that Rick would bring a needed professionalism and an outside leadership perspective to the camp to lead the organization into its next season of ministry.

Howard strongly disagreed with the decision, feeling that his sons had been overlooked, that the board should have at least hired someone familiar with the organization, and that he should have had a say in who would be the next general director. Brian and Dennis were also upset, not only that neither of them had been selected as the next director but also that neither had been named the official interim director after their father's retirement.

The board did not know, however, that during Anthony's tenure as interim director, Brian and Dennis subtly undermined his leadership when he was not present. The two sons cultivated a loyalist segment among the staff who supported the family's continued leadership of the camp. The rest of the staff members followed Anthony as the board's appointed interim director, awaiting the appointment of the new director, which, they hoped, would put the politicking to an end.

When Rick arrived, all staff members initially welcomed him and verbalized their support. However, within just a few months, as Rick began to implement some changes that he felt were needed to professionalize the organization and better protect it from liability, the rumblings began. The Thornton-led cadre didn't like that Rick was taking Camp JOY away from its loosely run, family feel. However, other staff members felt that these changes were long overdue, and they welcomed Rick's ideas and his leadership.

To the casual observer, the camp's programs appeared to continue as usual, but behind the scenes a rift was quickly growing between Rick and his supporters, and Brian and Dennis and their supporters. The divide extended beyond the workplace, because the staff members not only worked together but also their lives intersected and overlapped in multiple areas. Nearly all of them attended the same small church, which had been founded by previous staff members and met at the camp. They all lived near each other, their kids went to school together, they ran into each other at the small mobile home that served as the local post office, and they helped each other with life in the rustic northwoods environment with regular work bees to build and repair homes, chop and store firewood, and preserve garden produce for the winter months.

But the person who felt the divide most acutely was Howard's brother-in-law, Walter. He and his wife had faithfully ministered alongside Howard and his family for decades. Howard was viewed as the fun-loving founding father in the extended camp family, while Walter was the wise elder statesman, albeit with an ever-present twinkle in his eye. Howard did not like that

Walter did not support him. Conversely, Walter did not agree with Howard, Brian, and Dennis and their tactics. He respected Rick as the legitimately selected general director and felt that his brother-in-law and nephews should as well. And the conflict was not just professional; it had turned personal, dividing the families several generations down.

The situation simmered as Camp JOY headed into its second summer season with Rick at the helm. The board continued to back Rick, while Howard, Brian, and Dennis continued to sow seeds of division. Brian and Dennis openly contradicted Rick and blatantly disregarded his directives. Howard undermined Rick to longtime camp constituents, including financial supporters and pastors. The divide between the staff was widening as well, with approximately half of the staff in support of Rick, and the others scorning him in favor of the Thornton family.

Meanwhile, Rick grew discouraged and tired. He had no vendetta against the Thornton family and had never anticipated the divide and the opposition he was now facing. His repeated attempts at peacemaking were rebuffed. It seemed that the Thornton family and their supporters would be happy only if Rick were removed and one of them, perhaps even Howard out of retirement, were appointed general director.

QUESTIONS FOR REFLECTION

1. With the information you've been given, how would you summarize the problem(s) in this case?

2. Who are the main characters and what are their roles in this situation?

3. What assumptions and values do you hear voiced by these characters?

4. What other information do you wish you had about this situation?

5. What seem to be the technical challenges involved in this case?

6. What are the adaptive challenges, and what type of adaptive challenges are they?

7. What risks and opportunities do you see in this case?

8. What are biblical and theological principles that should be considered in this case?

9. What are your suggested next steps for the parties involved?

10. What longer-term considerations might impact short-term decisions?

11. What work should be given "back to the people" here? To whom, and how?

12. What are your own assumptions and values that guide your recommended course of action?

13. What responses did you notice within yourself as you read this case?

14. Do you think anything could have been done differently, either individually or organizationally, to avoid this situation? If so, what?

15. Might this case be different if:

    a) Howard's sons were not on Camp JOY's staff, or only one of them was?

    b) Walter supported Howard instead of Rick?

    c) Howard and Walter did not have decades of shared ministry?

16. Issues to consider:

    a) What are the ingredients of a successful leadership succession plan?

    b) What is the role of the board in cases of staff conflict? What about if there is open insubordination toward a designated leader?

    c) What are best and wise practices for a leader in relation to his or her organization and its new leadership upon retirement?

Commentary

Despite the board's ongoing affirmation of Rick as the general director, Howard and his sons continue to subvert his leadership and stir up division. Whereas the conflict was originally contained within Camp JOY's staff, it is now affecting the camp's financial bottom line as donors have reduced or stopped their giving and churches have threatened not to send groups depending on who is in charge.

To this point, the board has governed from a distance, meeting onsite several times a year and trusting the general director and staff to carry out the work of the camp's ministry. This is not an unusual arrangement in healthy organizations. However, the board will need to become more directly involved in the situation because there seems to be no easy solution in sight. Rick might be correct in his assessment that Howard, his sons, and his supporters will not be happy unless someone from the Thornton family is in charge. In a normal world, Rick or the board could remove Brian and Dennis from their staff roles. However, the divide is now so deep that a split may be inevitable, no matter who is general director.

Additional Questions

1. Has your initial diagnosis of this situation changed? If so, how and why?

2. Which character(s) do you find yourself empathizing with?

3. Do you need to revise or address any of your assumptions?

Epilogue

By fall, the board realized it needed to intervene. However, while the majority of the board members still supported Rick as general director, no one wanted conflict, and no one wanted to take action against anyone involved. At that point, the field opened for anyone to make a play for power. At a regularly scheduled meeting in November, one board member insisted that *he* become the director because of his longtime loyalty to the ministry and his previous nonprofit leadership experience. When the other board members voted down this idea, he stormed out of the timber lodge where the board was meeting. When several other board members followed him out, he cried and screamed at them, "I've worked too hard not to get this!" He resigned shortly thereafter.

Meanwhile, the Thornton faction of the staff dug in for a fight. They couched the conflict in spiritual terms, claiming that as founder, Howard was God's chosen man to continue to lead the camp. They held prayer meetings for "the good of the ministry," although staff who were known Rick sympathizers were not invited.

On a cold February morning, Rick was about to head to camp when he discovered that someone had slashed his tires. While the perpetrator was never found, everyone assumed it was a shot across the bow from someone in the Thorntons' camp.

In March, word got out that Howard was preparing to form a rogue board that would lead a hostile takeover of the ministry. These board members were longtime friends of Howard, many of them elderly men who had served on staff or on the board during Camp JOY's early days. Whether or not such a takeover was legal, many of the real board members were exhausted, tired of emergency meetings and of fighting the Thornton family. Rick was also tired and did not want the ministry, the staff, or his family to continue to suffer from the division.

Walter tried to engage his brother-in-law in one more conversation to plead for reconciliation and unity. Howard declined to give up his fight.

In mid-April, the rogue board scheduled a meeting in the Chicago area. Rick and his wife made the six-hour drive to meet with them, while Walter and Dorothy Larson convened a meeting of Rick's supporters at their house to await news from the meeting. For many of them, their lifetime of ministry at the camp and their livelihoods were at stake. They knew that if Howard's group succeeded in its takeover, they would no longer be welcome to remain on staff.

As the group prayed and waited pensively, Walter received a phone call from Rick. He had met with Howard and the rogue board, asking them not to continue to divide the ministry. When they declined, he offered his resignation in exchange for a generous severance package, an offer that was immediately accepted. Rick would no longer be the general director of Camp JOY. The legitimate board members also resigned, although several of them were soon asked to join the takeover group.

Walter reported the news, then addressed the stunned group assembled in his den. "Well, we asked God for clear direction," he said. "Let's thank God for answering our prayer." With that, he led the men and women in a tearful prayer, asking for God to continue to bless the camp, to give wisdom to every staff person, and to provide for them and their families. This was not how anyone in the room wanted the ordeal to end, but they were inspired by Walter's faith and courage to follow what he felt was the right path, even when it meant losing something he had spent a lifetime helping to build.

The following week, Brian Thornton was named as the new general director by the new board. Within another two weeks, eleven of the twenty missionary staff members—all those who had supported Rick—announced their resignations, effective by the end of May. The staff who remained, including Brian and Dennis, were angry with those who resigned because it left the camp exceedingly short-staffed heading into the busy summer season.

By the end of the summer, the eleven staff members who resigned had scattered around the country: to graduate school, to ministry at other camps, and to non-ministry jobs. Many never again set foot on Camp JOY's property or spoke with the Thornton family. Rick and his family moved west, where he became director of a smaller conference center in the Rocky Mountains.

Howard passed away five years after orchestrating the takeover. Walter died twelve years after Howard, after a valiant struggle with cancer. Brian served as general director for twenty-two years before retiring. Brian and Dennis's youngest brother has served on the board continuously since being part of the takeover group. Camp JOY now serves nine thousand campers per year at three sites.

⊣ NOW WHAT? ⊢

1. How do you feel now that you've read the entire case and know how it ended?

2. Would you have acted similarly?

3. How could a different result have been achieved?

4. What actions can you, your fellow leaders, and your organization take to prepare for—and perhaps avoid, mitigate, or replicate—this particular situation or outcome?

Recommended Resources

Bolman, Lee G., and Terrence E. Deal. *Reframing Organizations: Artistry, Choice, and Leadership.* 7th ed. San Francisco: Jossey-Bass, 2021.

Hanberg, Erik. *The Little Book of Boards: A Board Member's Handbook for Small (and Very Small) Nonprofits.* North Charleston, SC: CreateSpace, 2015.

Rothwell, William J. *Effective Succession Planning: Ensuring Leadership Continuity and Building Talent from Within.* 5th ed. New York: AMACOM, 2015.

CHAPTER

04 | HIGH OFFICE

Joel Madden was a prominent politician in a Bible-Belt state. A native son, Joel went to college and law school at the state university and stayed in town after graduation to begin his political career. Thirty-five years later, he was the picture of success: an icon in his state as a university legend, multiterm state politician, school board member, married father of two, and prominent member of First Christian Church, where he had served in a variety of leadership roles over the years, including Sunday school teacher, deacon, and member of multiple search committees for various pastoral and staff positions.

At age fifty-seven, Joel had just announced his intention to run for national office, launching his campaign with a video showing him shaking hands with senior pastor Robert Clayton on the front steps of First Christian Church. He was the quintessential "faith and family candidate," running on a campaign of character and Christian values.

Six months after beginning his campaign, a report was published saying that Joel had had an affair with a woman while he was visiting different parts of the state doing work related to his elected office. He first denied it vehemently, saying that the woman was a stalker and that the truth would come out soon enough. The next day, when asked by a reporter about the alleged affair, he strongly denied it again. However, the reporter then played him a recorded conversation with the woman in which the woman described their sexual activity in great and lurid detail. Joel then confessed to the affair and announced he was suspending his election campaign.

To complicate matters even further, Joel also admitted to an "inappropriate" encounter with a woman who had turned to him for advice regarding her broken marriage years earlier. At that time, he had gone through counseling and had talked to Robert Clayton about the situation, and no one else had known about it. Joel and his wife separated discretely for a time in the wake of that revelation but eventually reconciled. The more recent affair had gone on for several years before it became public knowledge after a reporter was tipped by a politician from a rival party.

The leaders at First Christian were stunned by Joel's confession and then by the disclosure of the previous relationship. As word quickly spread, congregants developed—and did not hesitate to verbalize—strong opinions. Many felt that Joel was the victim of a smear campaign by the opposing political party and could not possibly have done the things of which he had been accused, despite his confession. They could not believe his mistress would betray his trust, and they sympathized with Joel in his humiliation. Others felt that as long as he was effective at his political work and particularly for his party and its platform, he should not receive any consequences. Still others pointed to his long history of faithful involvement in the church and felt he should be granted grace for this most recent indiscretion.

Meanwhile, a quiet minority within the congregation felt deeply embarrassed that the church and their pastor had so staunchly supported a politician in the first place, and that now the church's reputation and witness were being dragged through the mud as a result of Joel's scandal. They held that his record of service and his political views should not exempt him from the same moral and leadership standards as anyone else in the church.

The elders debated about not only what to do but also how public their action and communication should be. Joel was prominent both inside and outside the congregation, beloved by some and reviled by others; a political hero and scapegoat, or a scumbag adulterer and liar. What's more, in the public eye Robert Clayton and First Christian Church were now also associated with the entire sordid affair. Whatever decision the elders made, it would have far-reaching, long-lasting consequences.

QUESTIONS FOR REFLECTION

1. With the information you've been given, how would you summarize the problem(s) in this case?

2. Who are the main characters and what are their roles in this situation?

3. What assumptions and values do you hear voiced by these characters?

4. What other information do you wish you had about this situation?

5. What seem to be the technical challenges involved in this case?

6. What are the adaptive challenges, and what type of adaptive challenges are they?

7. What risks and opportunities do you see in this case?

8. What biblical and theological principles should be considered in this case?

9. What are your suggested next steps for the parties involved?

10. What longer-term considerations might impact short-term decisions?

11. What work should be given "back to the people" here? To whom, and how?

12. What assumptions and values guide your recommended course of action?

13. What responses did you notice within yourself as you read this case?

14. Do you think anything could have been done differently, either individually or organizationally, to avoid this situation? If so, what?

15. Might this case be different if:

    a) Joel Madden were not affiliated with the "favored" political party within the church?

    b) Joel had disclosed the affair on his own?

    c) Joel's affair were revealed outside of an election cycle?

16. Issues to consider:

    a) What should be the relationship between a church and political parties? What about between a pastor or ministry leader and a political or other prominent figure?

    b) Should a church ever call attention to, celebrate, or boast about its famous members such as politicians, entertainers, or athletes?

c) Should church discipline be conducted any differently
for a member who is a public figure? What if the figure
is especially popular within the congregation?

Commentary

It is tempting to overlook the behaviors of a public figure who is part of our church or ministry, especially if we feel they are on the "good" or "right" side of a political or cultural battle or if they are publicly beloved. Leaders and congregants can also look to a celebrity's participation in our ministry as a source of pride or validation: "So-and-so goes to *our* church!" But these tendencies are in contradiction to the humility that Jesus talks about and is expanded on by the apostle James in his epistle.

Celebrity is a dangerous bedfellow for the church. In this situation, the leaders of First Christian Church will need to put aside their political preferences and partisanship and Joel's prominence and look at him as a sinful and mortal human being, just like anyone else in the congregation or in the church's leadership. What would be the church's normal course of disciplinary action in this type of situation? Will First Christian's leaders be willing to follow this course with this favored son?

ADDITIONAL QUESTIONS

1. Has your initial diagnosis of this situation changed? If so, how and why?

2. Which character(s) do you find yourself empathizing with?

3. Do you need to revise or address any of your assumptions?

Epilogue

It quickly became clear that a majority of the congregation supported Joel no matter what he had done. In the charged climate of an election season, the situation had become so politicized and emotionally explosive that many elders feared revolt and division within the church if they exercised any type of discipline with Joel. And truth be told, a number of the elders agreed with congregants that a win for Joel and his party was more important to the big picture, given the perceived stakes in this election.

Because the leadership could not reach a consensus, no further public action was taken. The congregation was largely satisfied and supportive by this course of (in)action, although a few members quietly departed. The majority of the pastors and staff involved in that decision, including pastor Robert Clayton, have since moved on from First Christian Church. Meanwhile, Joel Madden still holds a high-ranking state political office and continues to serve at the church. After another separation following the disclosure of the affair, he and his wife have again reconciled.

Now What?

1. How do you feel now that you've read the entire case and know how it ended?

2. Would you have acted similarly?

3. How could a different result have been achieved?

4. What actions can you, your fellow leaders, and your organization take to prepare for—and perhaps avoid, mitigate, or replicate—this particular situation or outcome?

Recommended Resources

Black, Amy E., gen. ed. *Five Views on the Church and Politics.* Counterpoints: Bible and Theology. Grand Rapids: Zondervan Academic, 2015.

Ward, Angie, gen. ed. *Kingdom and Country: Following Jesus in the Land That You Love.* Kingdom Conversations. Colorado Springs, CO: NavPress, 2022.

Whitehead, Andrew L. *Taking America Back for God: Christian Nationalism in the United States.* Oxford, UK: Oxford Univ. Press, 2020.

---

05 | IS IT ME?

Amanda Walker was a confident, competent forty-five-year-old woman with several decades of experience as an effective ministry leader, communications strategist, and leadership coach. For the past several months, she had been serving as a consultant to Cornerstone Christian Academy, an elite private Christian high school in an affluent suburb of a large metro area. Cornerstone had experienced rapid growth since its founding twelve years earlier, and the school's CEO and headmaster enlisted Amanda's help. Over six months, she engaged in a communications project that involved interaction with the school's top donors and various academic and administrative staff. The headmaster, Elliott Hoff, also sought her counsel about ways to support sustained performance and growth.

Based on her insights and recommendations as a consultant, Elliott recruited Amanda to join the organization in a staff role to implement her recommendations and align five functional areas within the organization. The plan was for Amanda to start in her staff role part-time that August, phasing up to full-time in November after she completed several other consulting contracts. Amanda would serve as a member of Cornerstone's executive team and report directly to Elliott, who in turn reported to Cornerstone's board of trustees.

Amanda had known Elliott twenty years, working on his team for several years at another organization before moving to other opportunities. Based on her previous experience, Amanda thought of Elliott as a nice guy with a sharp mind and big ideas, albeit somewhat socially awkward. However, within her first ninety days on staff at the school as Elliott's direct report, Amanda began to experience behavior from him that quickly raised several red flags.

During a one-on-one meeting with Elliott that October, Elliott reported that he had been hearing from other members of the executive team that Amanda had been acting more like a consultant than an employee. Amanda was caught off guard by this comment because she was in the ramp-up phase of her employment with Cornerstone and had just started to invest more time in relationships with the staff, including her group of fourteen direct reports.

While Amanda thanked Elliott for the feedback and told him she would reflect on it, she was alarmed that Elliott had promoted anonymous feedback. This ran directly counter to the organization's cultural expectations, detailed in a comprehensive twenty-three-page document, which were considered a hallmark of hiring and employment at Cornerstone. This vaunted document explicitly promoted a work culture with "no surprises" and no anonymous feedback. Employees were encouraged to have honest, transparent conversations. Yet in his meeting with Amanda, Elliott had flouted this standard.

Amanda decided that before her next meeting with Elliott, she would meet one-on-one with each member of the executive team to check in, asking each of them what they were seeing in her job performance and interactions, whether they could point out any blind spots, and for ongoing feedback to help her learn and grow. During those conversations, not one member of the executive team expressed the concerns Elliott had communicated. For Amanda, this experience dealt a significant early blow to her trust in Elliott. She wondered why Elliott now seemed resistant to a fellow leader who could engage with him as a subject-matter expert and bring her competencies to complement his.

This wasn't the only behavior that raised warning flags. Over time, Amanda also experienced negative behavior in the form of Elliott's not following up on things he had communicated; undermining of her authority, through both private conversations and overt overruling; insecurity about his legacy and who would get credit for leadership decisions; lack of empathy toward various individuals within the organization; and gaslighting by not seeming to remember significant conversations and decisions and questioning her memory when she asked for follow-through.

In her first months on the job, Amanda gave Elliott the benefit of the doubt, thinking perhaps it was her fault or responsibility as she adjusted to working inside the organization. To be fair, there were some good days and good exchanges when the pressure Amanda felt would ease. Elliott showed a great sense of humor and a strong instinct for strategy, and he made efforts to help Amanda feel welcome as she integrated with the executive team. He even praised some of the early wins she had guided her staff to accomplish.

But as she continued to reflect on the troubling encounters she experienced, Amanda realized the unhealth of her supervisor and of the entire system. Using her knowledge as an organizational consultant, she envisioned the situation in terms of a matrix depicting the level of challenge compared with the level of support for a leader.

If the level of challenge is low and the level of support is low, the result is usually apathy. If, on the other hand, the level of challenge is high and the level of support is high, the environment is often one of high performance. Low challenge combined with high support results in maintenance of the status quo.

It was an aha moment for Amanda to realize she was in an environment with high challenge but low support. She knew this type of environment is highly stressful and not sustainable for a leader or for her health. It also ran contrary to another section of Cornerstone's cultural document, which contained statements about working sustainably and choosing excellence over expedience.

Indeed, Amanda's health had started to suffer. As her body flooded with the stress hormone cortisol, she lost sleep, gained weight, and felt constant fatigue. She woke up dreading each workday. The stress weakened her immune system and compounded an infection. She felt anxious and frayed, constantly thinking about the situation, rehashing conversations, second-guessing herself, and wondering what she should do.

In addition to the personal impact, the situation affected Amanda's leadership of her team. When she started, she had several team members who were underperforming or the wrong fit for their roles. Some of them even demonstrated unethical behavior. She needed to hire their replacements but knew she would be bringing new employees into an environment that was not healthy, despite the espoused values of the organization. She also wondered how to cultivate trust with her team while managing the gap between productive and underperforming members in addition to the greater systemic dysfunction.

Amanda had accepted her position at Cornerstone thinking this could be a long-term role, with perhaps even a ten-year horizon for her tenure. But just halfway through her first year, she found herself seriously wondering how much good she could do, and for how long.

Questions for Reflection

1. With the information you've been given, how would you summarize the problem(s) in this case?

2. Who are the main characters and what are their roles in this situation?

3. What assumptions and values do you hear voiced by these characters?

4. What other information do you wish you had about this situation?

5. What seem to be the technical challenges involved in this case?

6. What are the adaptive challenges, and what type of adaptive challenges are they?

7. What risks and opportunities do you see in this case?

8. What biblical and theological principles should be considered in this case?

9. What are your suggested next steps for the parties involved?

10. What longer-term considerations might impact short-term decisions?

11. What work should be given "back to the people" here? To whom, and how?

12. What assumptions and values guide your recommended course of action?

13. What responses did you notice within yourself as you read this case?

14. Do you think anything could have been done differently, either individually or organizationally, to avoid this situation? If so, what?

15. Might this case be different if:

    a) Amanda were a man?

    b) Amanda had been hired by and directly reported to the board instead of to Elliott?

    c) Amanda were younger or less experienced?

16. Issues to consider:

    a) How does one determine whether a leader's behavior just needs a bit of extra grace or is dangerously unhealthy and detrimental to a team or an organization?

    b) How should a leader who is in a position under an unhealthy authority figure make concerns known, given the power dynamics at play?

    c) How does a leader know when a situation or environment has become too toxic to stay in it? What, if anything, does the leader "owe" the organization?

Commentary

While Amanda had not realized it and only a trained therapist can make an official diagnosis, Elliott demonstrates textbook signs of narcissism. The diagnostic criteria for narcissistic personality disorder state that an individual must demonstrate at least five of the following nine characteristics:

1. Has a grandiose sense of self-importance (e.g., exaggerates achievements and talents, expects to be recognized as superior without commensurate achievements).
2. Is preoccupied with fantasies of unlimited success, power, brilliance, beauty, or ideal love.
3. Believes that he or she is special and unique and can only be understood by, or should associate with, other special or high-status people (or institutions).
4. Requires excessive admiration.
5. Has a sense of entitlement (i.e., unreasonable expectations of especially favorable treatment or automatic compliance with his or her expectations).
6. Is interpersonally exploitative (i.e., takes advantage of others to achieve his or her own ends).
7. Lacks empathy: is unwilling to recognize or identify with the feelings and needs of others.
8. Is often envious of others or believes that others are envious of him or her.
9. Shows arrogant, haughty behaviors or attitudes.[1]

1. American Psychological Association, "Personality Disorders," in *Diagnostic and Statistical Manual of Mental Disorders*, 5th ed. (Washington, DC: American Psychiatric Publishing, 2013).

Amanda had ostensibly been invited into the organization by Elliott to make the changes that she had recommended and that he had confirmed. However, as she began to implement these changes, Elliott communicated concern that others might perceive the problems as being his fault. He wanted Amanda to deliver rapid solutions that would not implicate or embarrass him. She experienced particular difficulty with Elliott because her area of oversight was closely linked to Elliott's projected image as founder of the school, and almost any visible change would be perceived (and often opposed) by him as a smear on that image.

Amanda wants to do her job well in terms of both task completion and people management, but she must determine whether she will truly be able to do so given Elliott's resistance, the systemic dysfunction, and the toll the situation is taking on her health. She must also ascertain how much, or even whether, she can speak up about the overall system and what she has experienced. All of this is a lot for one leader to carry alone, so Amanda would be well served to find several people external to the situation who can provide support and a safe place to process what she is going through.

ADDITIONAL QUESTIONS

1. Has your initial diagnosis of this situation changed? If so, how and why?

2. Which character(s) do you find yourself empathizing with?

3. Do you need to revise or address any of your assumptions?

Epilogue

As the weeks and months went by, Amanda gained more clarity about the situation. A few years earlier, she had worked with a woman who demonstrated the traits of an overt narcissist. Amanda realized that the behaviors she experienced and observed with Elliott were almost identical, albeit more covert, more subtle, less grandiose. She had not yet entertained the label of narcissism for Elliott's behavior, but she realized Elliott was obsessed with his image and needed others to protect his self-esteem.

These realizations shaped how Amanda moved forward in relationship with Elliott, her team, and the organization. With Elliott, she began to use tactics practiced by those who work in hostage negotiation, communicating in ways that would not trigger defensiveness. She also used written communication more often as a prelude or recap to meetings with him, emailing him key highlights to protect against his later saying he didn't recall a discussion or decision. When Elliott used yes-no questions to pin her into a corner or a win-lose conversation, she tried to pivot the question to a middle-ground statement or a different take on the issue.

With her direct reports, Amanda began holding their regular group meetings in an isolated room, so conversations could not be overheard. She asked regularly how she could support them and modeled vulnerability about her own growth areas, building trust and a safe space for honest conversation. When she had to release staff members, she tried to be as clear and compassionate as possible. Eventually Amanda was able to hire new team members who were more qualified for the roles needed, although this had an unintended consequence: In addition to their enhanced competence in their jobs, these new employees were also more attuned to Amanda's stress and the dysfunction within the organization. This created additional tension for Amanda because she wanted to be a transparent leader while also maintaining confidentiality.

Within the broader organization, Amanda considered alerting the board to her concerns and Elliott's behaviors, but then decided against it after meeting with a couple of board members about other matters and realizing her credibility had been undermined.

During this season, Amanda found invaluable support in a faith-based mastermind group for women leaders she had joined before accepting her position at Cornerstone. She also leaned on several key friends and mentors and her husband. During her second year at the school, she began working with a leadership coach-counselor. She also regularly recorded her thoughts in a journal.

Meanwhile, Elliott continued to press her for faster progress toward various goals, including expectations beyond the detailed planning process of the executive team. When her conversations with Elliott did not seem to be getting through to him, Amanda decided to respond in writing, being as honest as she could be.

In a lengthy email, she explained that Elliott was asking for things that professionally she could not promise him and that his expectations were not sustainable based on her decades of career experience. Elliott did not respond favorably, blaming her for problems in the organization. At that point, Amanda realized that, although she had tried to be as truthfully kind and professional as possible, he was not able to receive her feedback.

Not long after that, Elliott asked all members of the executive team to review and update their job descriptions. Amanda provided him with a draft of her revised job description, but he did not agree with it, saying it showed too much emphasis on leadership and not enough on doing the work herself.

As the second school year progressed, Elliott's questionable behavior grew more and more overt. For example, he scrutinized Amanda's online calendar and quizzed her about the nature of her appointments and working time blocks. And after viewing her profile on a professional networking site, he asked if the articles she shared there were about him. By this time, Amanda was convinced Elliott had serious leadership flaws that seemed to be rooted in narcissistic behavior patterns. She saw no evidence of motivation to change, so it was time to craft an exit strategy.

Although Amanda's health continued to suffer, she decided to stay through the school year, which would give her team additional time together while also avoiding questions that might be raised about a midyear departure. Her last few months on the job were a slog to the finish line as she tried to inspire her team to keep pursuing excellence even while she was absolutely drained.

After leaving Cornerstone, Amanda engaged in conversations with close friends and leadership mentors, read books on narcissism and emotional health, and gained perspective in a few sessions with a therapist. All of these helped her process her experience, grieve the pain of it, and stop judging herself for not recognizing warning signs earlier. In addition, it took more than a year working with a functional medicine provider for Amanda to deescalate the stress in her body, eliminate her infection, and get on track to restored health.

Elliott left Cornerstone eighteen months after Amanda's departure.

NOW WHAT?

1. How do you feel now that you've read the entire case and know how it ended?

2. Would you have acted similarly?

3. How could a different result have been achieved?

4. What actions can you, your fellow leaders, and your organization take to prepare for—and perhaps avoid, mitigate, or replicate—this particular situation or outcome?

Recommended Resources

Cloud, Henry. *Necessary Endings: The Employees, Businesses, and Relationships That All of Us Have to Give up in Order to Move Forward.* New York: HarperCollins, 2011.

DeGroat, Chuck. *When Narcissism Comes to Church: Healing Your Community from Emotional and Spiritual Abuse.* Downers Grove, IL: InterVarsity Press, 2022.

Van der Kolk, Bessel. *The Body Keeps the Score: Brain, Mind, and Body in the Healing of Trauma.* New York: Penguin, 2014.

06 | WHO'S THE BOSS?

More often than not, leadership challenges do not present themselves as clearly and cleanly as in a written case study. Instead, information emerges piece by piece over a period of weeks, months, or even years. The following case is presented in this fashion. The situation began when the Cross-Cultural Missions Committee at First Evangelical Church began an extensive process of evaluating the church's cross-cultural missions philosophy, goals, and priorities. The following snippets include both points of fact and quotes from people involved in the situation. Imagine that you are a new elder at this church after attending for three years, and you must order these pieces as a newcomer to the situation. After you have read the facts, I suggest ordering them using the blanks to the left of each item or on a separate sheet of paper.

_____ First Evangelical Church was founded in November 1980.

_____ Approximately two hundred of the church's current attenders have been with the church for more than twenty years.

_____ The lay support and prayer group for missionaries is comprised primarily of members who have been with the church for more than twenty years.

_____ The church's original missions plan was to find people who were interested in missions, get them on the field overseas, and keep them there.

_____ In September 2016, a task force unanimously recommended to the elders that the new policy for selection and support of missionaries should be applied to current missionaries.

_____ In December 2018, the four selected missionary families received notice via letter that their financial support would be terminated at the end of fiscal year 2019 (June 30).

_____ There is intense mistrust from the lay support and prayer group toward the Cross-Cultural Missions Committee and toward the elders of the church.

_____ In September 2017, current missionaries were contacted and informed of the evaluation process and criteria.

_____ First Evangelical Church was founded in a university community that is pervaded by suspicion of formal authority.

_____ A member of the lay support and prayer group: "You can't just stop supporting our missionaries! That would be like a divorce!"

_____ In June 2016, a task force was formed to determine whether the new policy for selection and support of missionaries should be applied to current missionaries.

_____ A deacon at First Evangelical Church: "The church is obligated to good stewardship of its financial resources."

_____ In October 2017, Glenn Thompson stepped down from his position as volunteer pastor of cross-cultural missions. He was replaced by his handpicked and groomed successor, Kristi Young, who had attended the church since her freshman year of college.

_____ As First Evangelical Church has changed (up to 75 percent turnover over many years), the missions ministry has moved away from being a set of relationships that are embraced by the whole church. Instead, it has become based on personal relationships with a small group of members who have been a part of the community since the early days of the church.

_____ The church constitution states that both the agenda for the annual congregational meeting and the budget can be modified from the floor at the meeting.

_____ In 2012, Glenn Thompson, a former elder, became the volunteer pastor of cross-cultural missions, and chair of the Cross-Cultural Missions Committee.

_____ The church started with thirty members. It now has weekly attendance of more than 1,200 adults.

_____ In 2016, the pastor who succeeded the founding pastor was granted a change in title from Teaching Pastor to Lead Pastor.

_____ Throughout the evaluation process, the Cross-Cultural Missions Committee communicated privately with the church's missionaries, citing confidentiality. The committee was subsequently charged of secrecy by the lay support group.

_____ In April 2015, the Cross-Cultural Missions Committee, under the charge of the elders, drafted a document outlining the criteria for selection and ongoing support of cross-cultural missionaries for First Evangelical Church.

_____ In November 2018, the elders approved the task force's recommendation regarding the termination of support for four missionary families.

_____ In June 2019, there was a congregational meeting to vote on the proposed termination of support.

_____ In June 2018, the deacons at First Evangelical Church, facing a major budget shortfall, voted to make large cuts in the church's program budget and staff benefits, rather than lay off any staff.

_____ Of the church's current missionaries, none relies on the church for more than 20 percent of their annual support.

_____ At the 2017 annual congregational meeting, the elders presented their recommendation for consolidated pastoral leadership in the form of a title change for the functional lead pastor. It was questioned from the floor and never made it to a vote.

_____ The task force to evaluate current missionaries is chaired by William Turner, a former missionary and current elder who did not seek involvement on the committee but was asked for input because of his experience.

_____ In January 2011, the church's children's pastor was terminated for inappropriate emotional and physical conduct.

_____ The new criteria for selecting and supporting cross-cultural missionaries says that missionaries should be working with nationals to raise indigenous leadership and must be willing to account for funds provided by the church.

_____ There are several groups with an interest in this case: the elders; the minister for cross-cultural missions; the Cross-Cultural Missions Committee, chaired by

William Turner; and the lay support and prayer group.

_____ In September 2017, a new task force was formed to evaluate current missionaries under the new criteria.

_____ For the first thirty-five years of its existence, First Evangelical Church did not have a senior or lead pastor. The church's founding pastor was the teaching pastor, and decisions were made by the congregation.

_____ Glenn Thompson is a tall, articulate Caucasian male in his midfifties. Kristi Young is a short, casual Asian female in her midtwenties.

_____ In December 2018, the church's lead pastor resigned, citing God's direction to step down. The meeting to process this announcement with the congregation was led by the elders and met with acrimony by a vocal minority in the congregation.

_____ In October 2009, the church's founding pastor stepped down after a prior extramarital affair was exposed.

_____ In January 2019, a church town-hall meeting was held, at which it was announced that the policy change was actually a recommendation and not a final decision.

QUESTIONS FOR REFLECTION

1. What is the rough order and timeline of events in this case?

2. With the information you've been given, how would you summarize the problem(s) in this case?

3. Who are the main characters and what are their roles in this situation?

4. What assumptions and values do you hear voiced by these characters?

5. What other information do you wish you had about this situation?

6. What seem to be the technical challenges involved in this case?

7. What are the adaptive challenges, and what type of adaptive challenges are they?

8. What risks and opportunities do you see in this case?

9. What biblical and theological principles should be considered in this case?

10. What are your suggested next steps for the parties involved?

11. What longer-term considerations might impact short-term decisions?

12. What work should be given "back to the people" here? To whom, and how?

13. What assumptions and values guide your recommended course of action?

14. What responses did you notice within yourself as you read this case?

15. Do you think anything could have been done differently, either individually or organizationally, to avoid this situation? If so, what?

16. Might this case be different if:

   a) First Evangelical Church had not experienced the departure of several ministry leaders because of inappropriate behavior?

   b) The church were ten years old instead of more than
      forty?

   c) The church had attendance of three hundred instead of
      1,200?

17. Issues to consider:

   a) What, in your view, is the best balance of power
      between leadership and a congregation?

   b) What are the challenges of stereotypes regarding how
      a leader should look and act in terms of age, ethnicity,
      gender, height, mannerisms, and more?

   c) How can missional and operational values be
      communicated to newcomers, and to new leaders, as a
      church grows?

   d) What can be done to build or rebuild trust of leaders
      within an organization?

Commentary

First, a word about the format of this case. You probably felt disoriented and maybe frustrated as you read the snippets of information and tried to put them in some semblance of order. This is a normal response for a leader who is thrown into a situation with which she or he is not familiar. While it would have been easier to present this case as a linear narrative, it would have been less true to real life. When an adaptive challenge arises, a leader must usually piece together the backstory to see how the challenge emerged. And it is just plain hard leadership work to gather all the facts on the fly, to make sense of them, and to withhold judgment until enough information has been gathered to give the balcony view required for effective adaptive leadership.

First Evangelical Church operates in a cultural context where there is widespread mistrust of authority. This mistrust has been exacerbated organizationally by the indiscretions of previous leaders and facilitated by a governance system that functionally allows every individual member to hold veto power over any decisions by church leadership. While the church developed an initial philosophy about cross-cultural missions mobilization and funding, that philosophy was not codified or communicated to subsequent generations of lay leadership. As a result, there are now conflicting values between various groups of stakeholders, with no clear idea about who has authority to determine the path forward.

The leaders of First Evangelical Church must address both acute and chronic issues. In the short term, the elders must determine how to resolve the missions funding issue. In the long term, the church needs to acknowledge and work through its authority issues along multiple aspects, including emotional, spiritual, and structural. The real question is who will be given the authority to lead the congregation through this process.

ADDITIONAL QUESTIONS

1. Has your initial diagnosis of this situation changed? If so, how and why?

2. Which character(s) do you find yourself empathizing with?

3. Do you need to revise or address any of your assumptions?

Epilogue

As was stated in the snippets of the case, the elders of First Evangelical Church backtracked on their decision to change the policy regarding missionary funding, realizing that the church bylaws did not actually permit this type of unilateral decision-making, and instead clarified that it was a recommendation. The recommendation ultimately was followed, but on a slower time-table than originally suggested.

Meanwhile, the church had entered an interim season upon the resignation of its previous lead pastor, who departed partly out of frustration with the church's governance structure, which, he felt, hampered his ability to lead. During this interim period, First Evangelical Church enlisted the services of a consultant, who recommended a move to a team model of leadership. In this model, the emphasis was on the work of teams of lay volunteers, who were equipped for ministry by the staff and elders, under the leadership of a lead pastor. While the congregation seemed enthused about this model, several long-term elders felt that it took too much authority away from the board of elders, so these changes did not stick.

After an exhaustive twelve-month national search, at the end of 2019 the congregation of First Evangelical Church voted overwhelmingly to call a new lead pastor and to give him unprecedented leadership authority and latitude. Over the course of his continued tenure, this lead pastor has methodically led the church through sweeping changes, including a different theological framework, an updated constitution and bylaws, and a strong elder-led governance structure.

| NOW WHAT? |

1. How do you feel now that you've read the entire case and know how it ended?

2. Would you have acted similarly?

3. How could a different result have been achieved?

4. What actions can you, your fellow leaders, and your organization take to prepare for—and perhaps avoid, mitigate, or replicate—this particular situation or outcome?

Recommended Resources

Allison, Gregg R. "Part Four: The Government of the Church." In *Sojourners and Strangers: The Doctrine of the Church.* Wheaton, IL: Crossway, 2012.

Lewis, Tracy. *How to Write Articles, Constitutions, and Bylaws for Churches.* Independently published, 2019.

Johnson, Andy. *Missions: How the Local Church Goes Global.* Wheaton, IL: Crossway, 2017.

| MERGERS AND
ACQUISITIONS

GraceFull was a nondenominational church located in the south-central area of a city of approximately 400,000 people. Every week the church would set up a large gymnasium for weekly worship services. At its peak, GraceFull had approximately $650,000 in the bank and attendance of around 1,200 people each week. However, because of some internal problems, including a legal indictment of the executive pastor for financial malfeasance, many people left and attendance dipped to around five hundred per week. Still, the church had a strong core group that supported the lead pastor, Bruce Powell, and had a heart for outreach and missions.

Realizing the lead pastor was a shepherd-teacher, the elders team began to search for an associate pastor who could provide missional leadership from the "second chair" alongside the lead pastor. The new associate pastor, Garrett Moore, arrived with a mandate to help turn GraceFull around and restore it to growth and missional impact.

A year into Garrett's tenure, the elders decided to find a regular meeting spot rather than continue the labor-intensive weekly setup in the gymnasium. With their authorization and with plenty of money for a potential purchase, Garrett led a team through due-diligence investigation into various meeting spaces.

During this time, Bruce got together for coffee with Ethan Davis, the lead pastor of another area church, North Hills Fellowship. North Hills was a larger, older, and slightly more traditional church on the north end of town with attendance of around one thousand—and their own building.

"We're looking at buildings," Bruce reported.

"We've been thinking we should start a setup church down south and have two campuses," Ethan replied.

As the two men considered each other's resources, an idea quickly took shape. North Hills lacked financial resources and staff, while GraceFull lacked its own building.

"What if we merged?" they asked each other.

Both Bruce and Ethan went back to their elders teams and asked them to pray about a merger. All parties felt that this could be a unique opportunity. The two churches aligned theologically, and each had resources the other felt they lacked.

As part of the exploration process, GraceFull and North Hills engaged the input of a noted church-merger consultant. Both leadership teams read the consultant's book, read case studies from church mergers, and visited each other's services. The results were encouraging. As Garrett Moore reported, "We felt like, yeah, we could marry these people. How cool would that be, in a culture where churches split over theology and cultural differences, that we can say, 'Hey, let's come together for the kingdom'?"

The in-depth exploration process culminated in a week during which both congregations prayed for discernment, then the elders teams voted separately from each other on the same night. Both came to the same conclusion: it would be right and good to merge.

"I don't really have a theology of laying out a fleece," Garrett recalled, "but I will say that as I was sitting there hearing about the unified votes, I remember having this feeling that God was in this. It was the God moment you always hope to have." The new church was named Advent Community Church. The merger was approved in May with plans to officially become one church in September of that year.

The consultant was enlisted to lead both churches through the mechanics of the merger. It was decided that both sites would have live preaching, with service times staggered so that the designated preacher could drive back and forth between locations.

The biggest questions were who would be the lead pastor of the merged organization and what would the other lead pastor do? In what felt like a humble and generous move, GraceFull decided to fill the role of "acquired" church, even though it had greater financial resources. Similarly, GraceFull lead pastor Bruce Powell offered to become the missions pastor in the newly structured organization, ceding lead pastoral authority to Ethan Davis.

Both organizations were committed to a slow, deliberate merger process. Everyone had the best of intentions. Still, fissures began to appear after just a few months.

The first had to do with worship style. Both churches utilized similar song selections, but each performed them differently. GraceFull's style was more rock concert, while North Hills was mellower by comparison. However, the worship leaders were able to work through this friction and figure out how each campus could maximize its particular style and strengths under the new Advent banner.

The next sticking point that emerged was the children's ministry. Advent had committed itself to a multisite methodology of presenting a similar experience at each site. However, the children's ministry staff from the two merging churches had very different ideas of what that experience should be, and each felt their way was the best.

But the biggest difference was in leadership style between the staffs from the two churches. The leadership from GraceFull generally were more apostolic and driven toward outreach and missions, while the leaders from North Hills were pastor-shepherds. This caused increasing friction both individually and organizationally.

Meanwhile, although Bruce and Ethan spearheaded the merger conversation, neither was around during the actual mechanics of the merger because both took planned sabbaticals during the thick of the merger process. Their absences left both congregations without clear drivers during this critical time. Ethan returned first, to his agreed-upon role as lead pastor. When Bruce returned several months later, he quickly felt marginalized, even though it had been his choice to move out of the lead pastor role and into the missions pastor position. He had not anticipated how much of his identity would feel stripped away by making this change.

Then, just a few months after returning from his sabbatical, Ethan announced his departure from Advent. Five months later, Bruce resigned as well. Ethan moved into leadership coaching, while Bruce shifted to full-time ministry focused on foster care and adoption. The newly merged church was now without both of its previous lead pastors, who had been the two primary drivers of the merger.

QUESTIONS FOR REFLECTION

1. With the information you've been given, how would you summarize the problem(s) in this case?

2. Who are the main characters and what are their roles in this situation?

3. What assumptions and values do you hear voiced by these characters?

4. What other information do you wish you had about this situation?

5. What seem to be the technical challenges involved in this case?

6. What are the adaptive challenges, and what type of adaptive challenges are they?

7. What risks and opportunities do you see in this case?

8. What biblical and theological principles should be considered in this case?

9. What are your suggested next steps for the parties involved?

10. What longer-term considerations might impact short-term decisions?

11. What work should be given "back to the people" here? To whom, and how?

12. What assumptions and values guide your recommended course of action?

13. What responses did you notice within yourself as you read this case?

14. Do you think anything could have been done differently, either individually or organizationally, to avoid this situation? If so, what?

15. Might this case be different if:

    a) Neither church had felt they were lacking something in seeking a merger?

    b) Either church were part of a denomination?

16. Issues to consider:

    a) What are the most important questions and issues that should be considered when two churches are exploring a merger?

    b) What is involved in merging organizational cultures?

    c) How would you measure success in a merger of two organizations?

Commentary

GraceFull and North Hills have embarked on a journey that is becoming more common as churches look to join forces for various reasons, including maximizing shared resources, expanding missional impact, and staving off extinction. The idea of a merger sounds perfect on paper and theoretically can solve problems for both churches. But as this case demonstrates, a lot needs to be explored before signing an organizational marriage certificate.

The process of a true, healthy merger can take years. And it will work in the long term only if the leadership groups from each church do some deep organizational-culture excavation, digging below the surface issues of material and financial resources and even beyond the important questions of theological alignment.

Even when everything above the surface looks like an ideal match, the clash of organizational cultures can trigger seismic quakes that cause relational friction at best and can swallow the entire enterprise at worst. In reality, one of the churches usually ends up becoming the takeover organization, even if unintentional or nonhostile, while the other becomes the acquired organization.

In the case of the merger between GraceFull and North Hills, it seems that no one took the time to ask why the members of each church were driving past the other's building on a Sunday morning on their way to their chosen worship service. Clearly the attendees sensed bigger differences between the churches than just mechanics or even theology. The lack of understanding of organizational culture and its role in the merger is now creating unanticipated conflict in multiple areas.

In addition, a healthy merger of cultures requires wise, steadfast, and stable leadership. Now that both Bruce and Ethan have resigned during a time of growing turbulence, the chances of survival for the fledgling Advent Community Church have declined precipitously unless some other leaders step up and take responsibility for seeing the merger process through this difficult season and to full fruition.

ADDITIONAL QUESTIONS

1. Has your initial diagnosis of this situation changed? If so, how and why?

2. Which character(s) do you find yourself empathizing with?

3. Do you need to revise or address any of your assumptions?

Epilogue

Upon the departure of the two former lead pastors, the elders of Advent—a mix of leaders from the two congregations—appointed an executive leadership team including Garrett and two associate pastors. Still, without a senior pastor and with the staffs shuffled together, more and more conflict emerged. Elders and other leaders started to leave, followed by congregants. The executive team, remembering the God moment of the merger vote the previous May, continued to try to make the merger work. However, the departures continued with numerous staff saying they felt called elsewhere.

The board of elders ultimately decided that the church needed one individual to serve as lead pastor and enlisted a search firm to help identify and hire this person. Garrett applied for the position but was not selected. The search firm eventually identified three candidates for the lead pastor position. The elders quickly ruled out the first candidate and eventually eliminated the second candidate. However, when the third and preferred candidate withdrew his name from consideration, the elders went back and hired the second candidate, a man named Ricky Dolson.

Garrett resigned before Ricky's arrival, while the other two members of the executive team resigned within sixteen months of the start of his tenure. With attendance in continued decline, Advent decided to close the setup site that had previously been home to the GraceFull congregation. After five years, Ricky was asked to resign because of his authoritarian leadership style. He was replaced by Bryce Addison, who had been hired as executive pastor by Ricky.

Eight years after the merger attempt, Advent has regrown under its new leadership to attendance of more than one thousand people at weekend services at the former North Hills

Fellowship location. Only a few hundred of those attendees, and just a few staff members, were part of either of the original two churches.

NOW WHAT?

1. How do you feel now that you've read the entire case and know how it ended?

2. Would you have acted similarly?

3. How could a different result have been achieved?

4. What actions can you, your fellow leaders, and your organization take to prepare for—and perhaps avoid, mitigate, or replicate—this particular situation or outcome?

Recommended Resources

Kendrick, Klint C. *The HR Practitioner's Guide to Cultural Integration in Mergers and Acquisitions: Overcoming Culture Clash to Drive M&A Deal Value.* Mergers and Acquisitions Roundtable, 2022.

Schein, Edgar H. *Organizational Culture and Leadership.* 5th ed. Hoboken, NJ: Wiley, 2016.

Tomberlin, Jim, and Warren Bird. *Better Together: Making Church Mergers Work.* Expanded and updated. Minneapolis: Fortress, 2020.

08 | TRUST AND TRUTH

Norm Randerson couldn't believe the news, or the timing of it.

The mood at Grace Bible Chapel, where Norm Randerson was the pastor of leadership, was somber that morning in mid-September. Just a few days earlier, a gunman had opened fire at the mall, killing one person and injuring four others before being subdued by police officers. The incident made national news and shook the normally peaceful community in which Grace Bible Chapel was located.

But that wasn't the only difficult situation Norm was dealing with that weekend. A day earlier, two mothers had accused the children's pastor at Grace, Phil Manning, of inappropriately touching their daughters at a campfire during a recent children's ministry camping trip.

At the time, Grace Bible Chapel drew around 950 adult attendees each week from twenty-five miles in any direction. The children's ministry reached an additional two hundred children per week. Grace had recently come through the resignation of its long-time senior pastor after an extramarital affair; the new teaching pastor, Derek Adams, had been there for less than a year and was still learning the ropes in his new situation. In addition, the church had just moved into a beautiful new facility in August after a lengthy building project that had been interrupted by the senior pastor's disclosure and resignation.

Despite all this transition, the church had maintained its reputation as a respected congregation with far-reaching impact. It seemed like Grace was just beginning to make steps toward a new and exciting future, but now suddenly nothing seemed certain.

Because Norm oversaw the staff and had been at the church for more than twenty-five years, the chair of the board of elders, Tim Johnson, called Norm with the initial news. On Monday, September 17, Norm and Tim met with the two mothers—one who attended Grace, and one who didn't—to hear their stories.

According to the two mothers, they and their daughters were among a group of parents and children sitting around a campfire on a camping trip at a local state park. At different times during the evening, Phil had the mothers' girls on his lap, rubbing their bare arms and legs, presumably to help them warm up. The girls did not complain, but the mothers said they felt very uncomfortable observing Phil's actions. When asked why they did not speak up at the time, they said they didn't realize their shared feelings until they talked later, after the children had gone to bed.

Phil was a grandfatherly figure in his early fifties and had been on staff for ten years at the time of the allegations. He was a beloved figure to many in the church. Although he had been addressed in the past about some emotional-boundary issues such as special favor and gift-giving to certain children, there had never been an observation or complaint of inappropriate physical or sexual touch. The news was a shock.

In addition to the impact of Phil's behavior on the girls and their parents, not to mention on Phil and the congregation, Norm could not help thinking about the church's reputation in the community. He was not sure whether the mothers would file a police report or press charges, and whether such reports would be picked up by the local newspaper.

QUESTIONS FOR REFLECTION

1. With the information you've been given, how would you summarize the problem(s) in this case?

2. Who are the main characters and what are their roles in this situation?

3. What assumptions and values do you hear voiced by these characters?

4. What other information do you wish you had about this situation?

5. What seem to be the technical challenges involved in this case?

6. What are the adaptive challenges, and what type of adaptive challenges are they?

7. What risks and opportunities do you see in this case?

8. What biblical and theological principles should be considered in this case?

9. What are your suggested next steps for the parties involved?

10. What longer-term considerations might impact short-term decisions?

11. What work should be given "back to the people" here? To whom, and how?

12. What assumptions and values guide your recommended course of action?

13. What responses did you notice within yourself as you read this case?

14. Do you think anything could have been done differently, either individually or organizationally, to avoid this situation? If so, what?

15. Might this case be different if:

    a) Phil had not been addressed previously regarding his interactions with the children in his ministry?

    b) The two mothers and girls involved were both from within the church, or from outside the church?

    c) Grace Church had not just weathered a moral scandal with the affair and resignation of its former pastor?

16. Issues to consider:

    a) What is an organization's responsibility toward someone who makes allegations of inappropriate physical or sexual contact by a staff member? What is its responsibility toward the accused?

    b) What is the organization's obligation regarding truth-telling inside and outside the organization? What principles should guide what information is released, to whom, and when?

    c) What safeguards, such as policies and procedures, should be put in place within an organization to facilitate spiritual, emotional, and physical safety for all participants?

Commentary

Situations involving concerns of inappropriate physical or sexual contact are challenging enough for an organization that is relatively stable. Grace Bible Chapel is just finding its footing after a scandal involving its longtime senior pastor, the stress of a major building program and relocation, and the hiring of a new pastor. Now the church is about to be rocked again by the charges against its longtime children's pastor. Grace's leadership—with Norm Randerson viewed as the *de facto* pastoral leader because of his long tenure and steady presence through the upheaval of the past several years—must proceed carefully, considering a number of issues: First, they must investigate the charges more deeply; second, based on their findings, they must choose how to respond to the mothers and children, and what course of action they will take with Phil; and third, they must decide how, and how much, to communicate about the situation to the volunteers and families in the children's ministry, to the rest of the congregation, and to the community at large. Complicating this is the unknown of whether the mothers will somehow go public by filing a police report, pressing charges, or telling others in the community, and how any of these actions might impact the church.

Given all these factors and in light of the church's recent past, trust will be at a premium and potential landmines plentiful. How Grace's leaders respond—not just in what they do but in how they do it—will test their integrity and their witness, with potential long-term consequences.

| ADDITIONAL QUESTIONS |
---

1. Has your initial diagnosis of this situation changed? If so, how and why?

2. Which character(s) do you find yourself empathizing with?

3. Do you need to revise or address any of your assumptions?

Epilogue

The leadership board at Grace Bible Chapel quickly and unanimously placed Phil on a paid leave of absence while they investigated the situation. Some of the members of this board had also served in leadership roles during the moral failure of the previous senior pastor and the ensuing fallout, and they were determined to act deliberately yet expeditiously in this new situation.

In less than a week, it became clear that Phil had demonstrated a verifiable pattern of inappropriate behavior with children for many years. None of the instances seemed to rise to the level of criminal offense; however, the board was deeply concerned by the lack of wisdom and awareness of a staff member and in particular the children's director, and by the fact that this was a pattern and not a few isolated incidents. When confronted about these interactions, Phil did not seem to think that these behaviors were problematic, which the board also found concerning. In consideration of these factors and again acting in unity, the board came to the sad and regretful decision that Phil needed to be released from his position. In their eyes, Phil did not demonstrate the maturity needed by a person of his age and his position.

Meanwhile, people at Grace Bible Chapel were asking questions about why Phil had been placed on leave. The board communicated that there would be a congregational meeting in ten days to discuss the situation. However, they knew that those in attendance would want more information than the board would be able to give, that "lack of maturity" would be hard to quantify, and that a good number of congregants would back Phil, no matter what he had done. He simply came across as a likeable, sweet man, one who could not possibly be the bad guy. The board was confident in its decision and prepared for the blowback. But the board also wanted to be truthful without compromising confidentiality or disparaging Phil's Christian character.

Throughout this process, Norm communicated with the mothers who had registered their concern, informing them of the board's process and decision. One of the mothers filed a police report immediately after the event, describing the incident and expressing her concern, but she did not press charges because there did not seem to be criminal behavior. Overall, the women seemed satisfied that Grace Bible Chapel's leadership took their concerns seriously, and they did not want to smear the church's reputation. However, the police report would surely be noticed by the local newspaper. But as it turned out, the camp where the incident occurred was located in a different county than where Grace Bible Chapel was located, so even though the incident occurred just thirty minutes away from the church, the report was never noticed or picked up by the media in the church's home community.

Norm took the lead at the congregational meeting, which to no one's surprise drew a large crowd. Standing in front of the seated board—including new pastor Derek Adams—and drawing on his twenty-five years of relational capital and his pastoral presence, Norm explained that there had been concerns raised about Phil's interactions with children, including a recent incident. Norm did not provide details of that incident or of the others that the board interviews had uncovered, and explained that he and the other board members would not and could not do this. However, the fact remained that there were enough concerns that the decision had been made to release Phil from his position, effective immediately, although he would receive three months' severance pay. Norm then opened the floor to questions.

As expected, the response from those in attendance at the meeting was mixed. Many congregants just sat and listened, a few nodding in apparent agreement. Some asked for more details about the reported offenses, their posture and tone ranging from respectful to more forceful, even combative. The latter were part of a vocal minority who were visibly angered by the decision to terminate Phil's employment. They charged the board with hiding information and making up stories, and of making a big deal out of what were surely small or isolated incidents, simple indiscretions. They accused the board of doing the same thing with the previous pastor, even though he had confessed publicly to his behavior. The group pointed to Phil's longtime faithful service and his kind spirit and argued that the punishment did not fit the supposed crime. Some demanded to see the board's interview notes. Although these accusations hurt, the board was patient and gracious but resolute, the chairman reiterating Norm's talking points.

While on the outside Norm was poised and professional, on the inside he was hurting deeply. Norm loved this congregation. It pained him that not everyone would agree with the board's decision or with how it was enacted and communicated. He hated that his integrity was being called into question, including by some he considered to be longtime friends. Yet even more, it pained Norm to have to agree that his longtime friend and colleague needed to be dismissed from Grace's staff. Norm had seen a lot in his years of ministry; between the former pastor's moral failure and now Phil's dismissal, he had felt more disappointment, sadness, and sometimes anger than he had ever wanted to experience.

In the weeks and months after the meeting, several families left Grace Bible Chapel, citing lack of trust in the leadership. An interim children's minister was hired from within the ministry's volunteer ranks, and the interim tag was removed before the start of the next school year. Meanwhile, the new building and new location, along with the new pastor's skilled preaching, drew hundreds of new attendees to Grace Bible Chapel. Within two years, attendance had jumped to nearly 1,500 per week, and very few of those knew about Phil. Meanwhile, Phil and his wife, still professing his innocence, quietly and sadly left Grace Bible Chapel and began attending another church in a nearby town.

Norm served on staff at Grace Bible Chapel for nine more years before retiring.

Now What?

1. How do you feel now that you've read the entire case and know how it ended?

2. Would you have acted similarly?

3. How could a different result have been achieved?

4. What actions can you, your fellow leaders, and your organization take to prepare for—and perhaps avoid, mitigate, or replicate—this particular situation or outcome?

—————————— **Recommended Resources** ——————————

Covey, Stephen M. R. *The Speed of Trust: The One Thing That Changes Everything.* New York: Free Press, 2006.

MacDonald, Gordon. *Rebuilding Your Broken World.* Nashville: Thomas Nelson, 2004.

McKnight, Scot, and Laura Barringer. *A Church Called TOV: Forming a Goodness Culture That Resists Abuses of Power and Promotes Healing.* Carol Stream, IL: Tyndale Momentum, 2020.

SHOULD WE STAY OR SHOULD WE GO?

Carey Community Church (CCC) was founded near the downtown of a midsized city in 1987. Named after the famous English missionary to India, CCC was devoted to biblical teaching, foreign missions, and close fellowship among its members, under a congregational polity. After its first ten years, the leaders and congregation chose to relocate to a new four-acre facility situated near the western edge of the city near a major intersection running both north-south and east-west. The new facility had a worship center that seated three hundred, significant space for Christian education, a kitchen, a fireside room, and a gym with a full-length basketball court. Parking was more than adequate, and in 2002 the church hired thirty-seven-year-old Ron Atwater as its new senior pastor.

Over the next eight years, CCC grew from three hundred to five hundred attenders on Sundays with a diverse age range running from the elderly to more than sixty middle- and high-school students. Younger families had also started to attend, along with almost fifty college- and career-aged singles. In addition to Ron Atwater, the pastoral staff included a part-time children's minister, two part-time seminary students for the respective youth ministries, and a full-time director of Christian education. Giving was healthy and the mortgage on the new facility was being paid down earlier than anticipated.

However, by that time the surrounding neighborhood had also undergone a significant demographic change. Anglos had started selling their homes and moving to the suburbs as Hispanics moved into the area. And following unrest in southeast Asia there was an influx of refugees: thousands of Burmese refugees moved to a complex of low-rent apartments less than two miles from CCC. Moreover, it became clear that the majority of CCC people who had come to the church since 2003 were now driving in from the suburbs. Some younger staff and deacons, driven by the Christian-education director's strong emphasis on the Great Commission, began to press Pastor Ron to focus the church's outreach on the new people groups making up the neighborhood by hiring a Hispanic or an Asian pastor. Meanwhile, those driving in from the suburbs began to float the idea of building a new facility out on the new highway that ran right past the suburban development.

But as talk circulated among the members and staff of either hiring a new minister to reach out to the minority communities or selling the facility and building a new, expanded one toward the suburbs, tensions in the congregation grew. The older members of the congregation, led by deacon Donald Sutton and trustee Carl Kramer, felt strongly that these new ideas were disruptive to CCC's ministry and should be resisted at all costs. Meanwhile, another group of congregants and leaders wanted neither to change nor to move. They felt they had spent the last quarter-century building the current facility and ministries, and neither should be up for discussion.

Pastor Ron recognized that CCC as a whole was not staffed

or motivated to minister to its changing community. And as parents of four children, he and his wife identified strongly with all the new families who had come to the church over the prior five years and who pressed for the church to relocate. In an attempt to promote church unity, Ron started a preaching series on Romans 13–15. Some in the congregation felt he was pandering to the "old crowd" and left for a growing church in the southwest section of the city. Those in the congregation who sided with Donald and Carl resisted any idea of outreach to the Asian and Hispanic communities and were strident in their refusal to support a relocation. Following the departure of the Christian education director to a new ministry in a neighboring state, attendance dropped by more than one hundred people and the budget got tight. Ron knew that both he and Carey Community Church were at a crossroads as he tried to discern God's will for the future of the church and for himself as its pastor.

QUESTIONS FOR REFLECTION

1. With the information you've been given, how would you summarize the problem(s) in this case?

2. Who are the main characters and what are their roles in this situation?

3. What assumptions and values do you hear voiced by these characters?

4. What other information do you wish you had about this situation?

5. What seem to be the technical challenges involved in this case?

6. What are the adaptive challenges, and what type of adaptive challenges are they?

7. What risks and opportunities do you see in this case?

8. What biblical and theological principles should be considered in this case?

9. What are your suggested next steps for the parties involved?

10. What longer-term considerations might impact short-term decisions?

11. What work should be given "back to the people" here? To whom, and how?

12. What assumptions and values guide your recommended course of action?

13. What responses did you notice within yourself as you read this case?

14. Do you think anything could have been done differently, either individually or organizationally, to avoid this situation? If so, what?

15. Might this case be different if:

    a) CCC had a noncongregational form of government?

    b) The area were undergoing regentrification with an influx of wealth instead of a loss of it?

    c) Ron had been at the church longer or if he was older?

16. Issues to consider:

a) Does church unity need to take precedence over the Great Commission? If so, when and what does that look like?

b) What is the responsibility on the senior pastor and staff when lay leaders disagree with them about the direction of the church?

c) What values might a church codify and communicate about its mission? What should remain open and flexible?

Commentary

Carey Community Church faces questions not uncommon to churches in areas with demographic turnover: When the population surrounding a church changes, does the church follow its previous population, or does it reorient itself to reach its new neighbors? Does a church exist for a particular neighborhood or for a particular demographic?

The challenge facing CCC will expose several foundational questions. First, what are the church's values pertaining to missions and how do those relate to location? Second, who truly holds the authority and power within the church? Is it Ron Atwater, the senior pastor? Is it Donald Sutton and Carl Kramer, who hold secondary positions of formal authority yet, by virtue of their longevity, have significant influence within the congregation? Is it the younger staff members and lay leaders with their energy and enthusiasm for new ways of ministry? Or is it the congregation, who will ultimately vote to decide the future of the church? And what if that congregation is divided in its opinion?

| ADDITIONAL QUESTIONS |

1. Has your initial diagnosis of this situation changed? If so,
   how and why?

2. Which character(s) do you find yourself empathizing with?

3. Do you need to revise or address any of your assumptions?

Epilogue

As it turned out, Ron couldn't win. His attempts to foster unity
were viewed by both old and new attendees as a vote for the
other side. Following his series on Romans 13–15, the (old guard)
deacons and trustees unanimously asked for Ron's resignation.
Within a month, he departed to a new parish in another state.
The children's pastor, new part-time youth pastor, and newly
hired Christian education director stayed on while the church
brought in a local Bible college professor as their interim pastor. Within nine months, the church hired a sixty-two-year-old
veteran pastor from an ultraconservative background. Three
months after that, the new pastor fired the youth pastor for what
he termed a disrespectful attitude. The Christian education
director left of his own accord within a year.

The new senior pastor worked for four years and retired.
CCC went from about three hundred people to less than 175
under his tenure. In the year after his retirement, a new Christian
education director was hired to bring spiritual renewal, but he
moved on after two years. The church eventually declined to
fewer than sixty congregants and changed its name. After hiring
a series of senior pastors—none of whom brought renewal or

numerical growth—the church turned its facility over to a combination of two parachurch ministries and another small church that incorporated the remnant of CCC congregants, including Donald and Carl.

NOW WHAT?

1. How do you feel now that you've read the entire case and know how it ended?

2. Would you have acted similarly?

3. How could a different result have been achieved?

4. What actions can you, your fellow leaders, and your organization take to prepare for—and perhaps avoid, mitigate, or replicate—this particular situation or outcome?

Recommended Resources

Bird, Michael, and Brian Rosner, eds. *Mending a Fractured Church: How to Seek Unity with Integrity.* Bellingham, WA: Lexham Press, 2015.

Hagley, Scott. *Eat What Is Set Before You: A Missiology of the Congregation in Context.* Skyforest, CA: Urban Loft Publishers, 2019.

Strong, Mark E. *Who Moved My Neighborhood? Leading Congregations through Gentrification and Economic Change.* Downers Grove, IL: InterVarsity Press, 2022.

SOMETHING'S NOT RIGHT, PART 1

Ted Lewis was the pastor of discipleship and missions at Lighthouse Church, a nondenominational congregation in the suburban community of North Park. In his first few years after arriving at Lighthouse, the fifty-year-old had brought palpable energy and movement both to areas of ministry and, in particular, to the church's missions efforts, both locally and abroad.

Following a template he had used at a previous church, Ted initiated a hugely successful Christmas outreach event—an experiential movie night—that mobilized dozens of congregants as volunteers and brought hundreds of community members through the church's doors. Ted also increased foreign missions and awareness efforts, coordinating teams and reciprocal relationships between Lighthouse Church and ministries in the Caribbean, Africa, and the UK.

But Ted's crowning work was the formation of a basketball ministry that built on his experience and credibility as a former women's Division I college basketball coach to provide coaching, camps, and leagues to girls ages eight to eighteen. In the sports-crazy North Park community, Park Pride experienced explosive growth and rapidly gained a stellar reputation for developing both skill and character in its participants. The success of Park Pride and the other outreach programs led Lighthouse to enthusiastically undertake a successful capital campaign to upgrade Lighthouse's well-maintained but somewhat dated facilities.

Still, something wasn't quite right.

While Ted's ministries appeared successful by any external measure and he was a respected figure in the community, at church he was difficult to work with. In meetings with staff or elders he often came across as aloof, even disengaged, often engrossed in his laptop during discussions. He seemed to "misremember" conversations, thinking he was owed more—including compensation, preaching opportunities, and organizational authority—than others remembered promising, which contributed to an ongoing self-perception that he was chronically beleaguered.

Although he and his wife hosted the annual Lighthouse staff Christmas party, he became enraged when several coworkers tried to play a practical joke and temporarily repositioned some Christmas decorations from the extensive collection displayed throughout the Lewis house.

In addition to his disengagement and disgruntlement in leadership contexts, Ted did not seem to be a part of any regular relational community, even though staff were supposed to be active participants in one of the church's many small groups. His demeanor made a few in the church uncomfortable in a way that was difficult for them to quantify. However, for Ted's first five years at Lighthouse most of the congregation accepted him as just an odd duck, an overall good guy with a nice family who worked hard at his many roles.

In the church offices, though, many fellow leaders were growing tired of Ted's prickly persona. They experienced Ted as emotionally unhealthy and unaware, not a team player, resistant to community and accountability. He could be playful at times but grew moody and unpredictable. He increasingly gave the impression, even from the platform in the weekly worship service, that he would rather be somewhere else.

Complicating this situation was the church's leadership structure. Seven years earlier, Lighthouse had experienced a leadership crisis when it became apparent that the former senior pastor, Gary Nicolae, had been leading with an increasingly authoritarian hand. The issue was discovered when Gary, without documentation, due process, or notification of the elders, had fired the worship pastor one week before Christmas, then announced he would be taking a six-month sabbatical at the start of the new year.

During that time, the board of elders began to interview other staff—whom Gary had threatened with potential termination for insubordination if they participated in these conversations—and uncovered a pattern of bullying behavior. While Gary and the elders came to mutual agreement that his time at Lighthouse needed to end, many of the leaders at the church were wary of repeating the past by simply hiring a new senior pastor. Instead, the church moved toward a team leadership structure with no senior or lead pastor by design. The pastoral team was to include three members, including a pastor of discipleship and missions, a pastor of teaching ministries, and a pastor of worship and communication, all of whom would report to the board of elders. The elders, meanwhile, led by consensus, meaning they had to work toward a mutually supported decision.

Ted had been the first pastor hired into the new structure. He was joined fifteen months later by Peter Garcia as pastor of teaching ministries, and eighteen months after that by Chip Hogue, pastor of worship and communication. While all three had been hired as equal team members, Ted often claimed seniority because he had been the first hired. Peter, meanwhile, was viewed by many in the congregation as the senior pastor, because as pastor of teaching ministries he was the main preacher and platform presence.

Although Peter and Chip grew increasingly frustrated by Ted's behavior, neither had the authority to make an employment decision, although Peter had begun to restrict Ted's preaching opportunities given the latter's recent demeanor onstage and a decline in sermon preparation and therefore sermon quality. Under Lighthouse's structure, the elders held authority over pastoral staff, but they were divided in their opinion of Ted. Some volunteered within his ministry areas and had a rosier view of his job performance, while others had a history of personal run-ins with Ted or felt that interpersonal dynamics were as important to job performance as external growth. Still others felt strongly that pastors should never be fired except in the case of moral failure or financial malfeasance, and there was no evidence of either in this situation.

Meanwhile, the internal leadership tension increased with Ted growing sullener and Peter and Chip growing more convinced than ever that a change needed to be made, but uncertain as to how that change might take place given the church's leadership structure and differing values.

QUESTIONS FOR REFLECTION

1. With the information you've been given, how would you summarize the problem(s) in this case?

2. Who are the main characters and what are their roles in this situation?

3. What assumptions and values do you hear voiced by these characters?

4. What other information do you wish you had about this situation?

5. What seem to be the technical challenges involved in this case?

6. What are the adaptive challenges, and what type of adaptive challenges are they?

7. What risks and opportunities do you see in this case?

8. What biblical and theological principles should be considered in this case?

9. What are your suggested next steps for the parties involved?

10. What longer-term considerations might impact short-term decisions?

11. What work should be given "back to the people" here? To whom, and how?

12. What assumptions and values guide your recommended course of action?

13. What responses did you notice within yourself as you read this case?

14. Do you think anything could have been done differently, either individually or organizationally, to avoid this situation? If so, what?

15. Might this case be different if:

    a) Lighthouse Church had a senior pastor?

    b) Ted Lewis had not experienced as much outward ministry success?

c) Lighthouse Church were part of a clear denominational structure?

16. Issues to consider:

a) What are the strengths and weaknesses of a shared or team model of church leadership?

b) How much weight should interpersonal skills or emotional health be given versus ministry competence in an employee? Public self versus private self? External perception versus internal?

c) Should factors such as those in question 16b be included in a job description? If they are part of a job description, how should performance in these areas be assessed?

Commentary

Lighthouse Church is an example of an organization that, in an effort to mitigate problems stemming from a previous leadership structure, has overcorrected to a new structure, but into a different set of problems. In this case, it is unclear who will—or is allowed to—take the lead on addressing concerns regarding Ted Lewis's behavior. While the board does not need to be unanimous, they do need to reach consensus, and it appears there may not be consensus about the problems, their significance, and solutions. It is not clear how to fire a pastor at Lighthouse Church and what constitutes a fireable offense.

In addition, Ted's perception of miscommunication or misunderstanding, even if he is the one misremembering, indicates there has not been consistent, clear, firm communication and accountability by all parties across several years of natural board turnover. This includes communication to Ted, communication to new elders about past decisions, and consistent follow-through on those decisions by the current elders, who may have different perspectives about the decisions of previous boards of elders.

Until clear values have been established or unless there is a clear breach of an existing policy, the staff and the board will continue to spin their wheels, unable to move forward regarding this issue. Meanwhile, Ted's behavior will continue to erode team unity and morale and potentially even job satisfaction for his coworkers. They will each have to decide how long they will put up with his attitude and actions and how they will respond to each instance.

Additional Questions

1. Has your initial diagnosis of this situation changed? If so, how and why?

2. Which character(s) do you find yourself empathizing with?

3. Do you need to revise or address any of your assumptions?

Epilogue

Peter and Chip huddled regularly to figure out how they might take action. Initially, each spoke individually to Ted and then both spoke with him together as the whole of the pastoral team. Each time, their concerns were met with a few small behavioral changes that quickly reverted to previous patterns. Peter and Chip heard from other staff members who wondered what was going on with Ted. In light of growing concern, the two pastors strategized a formal charge to the elders regarding Ted's behavior, which was now beginning to affect not only internal interactions but also his external ministry effectiveness. However, Peter was not confident that the elders would be able to come to consensus regarding the situation.

It was near the end of the calendar year, and the leaders at Lighthouse were occupied with the usual flurry of Christmas activities. In the new year, several elders would rotate off the board and new ones would be added, potentially bringing new perspectives and a fresh opportunity for Peter and Chip to voice their concerns. For now, though, it was business as usual, albeit under an increasingly gloomy cloud.

Now What?

1. How do you feel now that you've read the entire case and know how it ended?

2. Would you have acted similarly?

3. How could a different result have been achieved?

4. What actions can you, your fellow leaders, and your organization take to prepare for—and perhaps avoid, mitigate, or replicate—this particular situation or outcome?

Recommended Resources

Brand, Chad Owen, and R. Stanton Norm, eds. *Perspectives on Church Government: Five Views of Church Polity.* Nashville: B&H Academic, 2004.

Cladis, George. *Leading the Team-Based Church: How Pastors and Church Staffs Can Grow Together into a Powerful Fellowship of Leaders*. San Francisco: Jossey-Bass, 1999.

Lencioni, Patrick. *The Advantage: Why Organizational Health Trumps Everything Else in Business*. San Francisco: Jossey-Bass, 2012.

SOMETHING'S NOT
RIGHT, PART 2

It was January, and Lighthouse Church, like many other churches, was returning to full speed after a post-Christmas lull. Ministry leaders came back to the office with new energy for the new year—except for Ted, that is. He continued to withdraw not only emotionally but also physically, showing up late for meetings, rejecting Sunday-morning responsibilities, even disappearing entirely during worship services. Several other staff members reported seeing Ted huddled over his computer in his office on Sunday mornings.

Meanwhile, Peter and Chip had grown resolute in their conviction that Ted needed to go. He had become a toxic presence within the organization, and they felt that this type of behavior must be addressed. The elders met twice per month, so in January Peter and Chip began to lay the foundation for a formal presentation at one of the meetings in February.

As they outlined the issues on paper, they realized how much time Ted was spending on his computer. "What is he doing in his office all the time?" Peter wondered aloud one Monday morning, after Ted had disappeared yet again during Sunday services. "Is there a way to check our network to see what he's doing on his computer?" he asked Chip.

Chip had a sudden realization: "I can check his internet usage!" As pastor of worship and communication, his responsibilities included oversight of the church's technology. This also gave him access to each staff member's computers and data. Chip called the church's tech person—a Christian who attended another church in the area—and asked for a report of activity from all church computers. Within a few hours, he received a call from the tech guy. "This is not good," the man told Chip.

The computer activity reports showed that Ted had been visiting adult chat rooms via his church-provided laptop during work hours, including Sunday-morning worship services. The activity had been going on regularly for months.

Peter and Chip were stunned as they looked at the report. This explained a lot of Ted's behaviors, and the problems were much worse than they had anticipated.

The two pastors immediately called the chair of Lighthouse's board of elders to let them know what they had just learned. They also printed the activity report and showed it to the church's executive administrator, who was also a member of the board of elders and a wise statesman in the church.

By that evening, the executive committee of the board had decided Ted needed to be put on administrative leave of absence. The following morning after a worship-planning meeting, the chair of the board arrived to read a prepared statement to Ted, announcing that he was being put on leave pending an investigation. Ted was immediately to hand in his keys, laptop, and church credit card, which he did without incident.

Once Chip had possession of Ted's laptop, he discovered more troubling activity, including frequent visits to gay hookup sites and searches for local hotels, some as recent as the previous week. Chip reported this information to the elders chair, who scheduled an emergency meeting of the full board of elders for the next night. They had some significant decisions to make.

Questions for Reflection

1. With the information you've been given, how would you summarize the problem(s) in this case?

2. Who are the main characters and what are their roles in this situation?

3. What assumptions and values do you hear voiced by these characters?

4. What other information do you wish you had about this situation?

5. What seem to be the technical challenges involved in this case?

6. What are the adaptive challenges, and what type of adaptive challenges are they?

7. What risks and opportunities do you see in this case?

8. What biblical and theological principles should be considered in this case?

9. What are your suggested next steps for the parties involved?

10. What longer-term considerations might impact short-term decisions?

11. What work should be given "back to the people" here? To whom, and how?

12. What assumptions and values guide your recommended course of action?

13. What responses did you notice within yourself as you read this case?

14. Do you think anything could have been done differently, either individually or organizationally, to avoid this situation? If so, what?

15. Might this case be different if:

   a) Ted Lewis's ministry focused on adults instead of teenage girls?

   b) Ted were not married?

   c) Ted had conducted his activity on his personal computer and not during work hours?

16. Issues to consider:

   a) Where are the lines between confidentiality and transparency, truth and slander when communicating to a congregation and other constituents about a leader's indiscretions and sins?

   b) What is the difference between a decision or process that is punitive, and one that is redemptive?

   c) Which constituencies are most important when determining the course of action in a situation such as this?

   d) Does the information in part 2 of this case cause you to rethink any of your perspective on the situation described in part 1?

Commentary

The elders at Lighthouse Church are faced with momentous choices—not just about Ted's future but about how decisions are communicated and carried out. These choices will have deep and lasting impact on Ted, his wife and children, the church, and the families served by the basketball ministry, among others. Based on how this situation is handled, Lighthouse and its leadership could gain or lose credibility and Christian witness almost overnight. The leadership could also expose the church to legal action and long-term financial consequences.

Lighthouse's leadership structure requires consensus to make a decision. Given the many factors at play and previous reluctance to take action, it is not a given that the elders will come to agreement. One thing is certain, however: Lighthouse's values and shared leadership model will surely be put to the test in the days and weeks ahead.

ADDITIONAL QUESTIONS

1. Has your initial diagnosis of this situation changed? If so, how and why?

2. Which character(s) do you find yourself empathizing with?

3. Do you need to revise or address any of your assumptions?

Epilogue

The elders met in emergency session on Wednesday night, two days after Ted's computer activity was discovered. Both Peter and Chip, as pastoral members of the board of elders, were in attendance. The elders chair asked them to present their findings to the board and then instructed the members to go home, consider the information, and pray before returning for another board meeting the next evening.

When the elders reconvened on Thursday night, they all agreed that Ted needed to be released from employment at Lighthouse and that the church should care for Ted and his family. However, there was significant disagreement on what should be communicated. Should Ted be fired without a statement to the congregation or to the basketball community? If there was to be communication, what information should it include? Several members of the board were concerned about the potential of a lawsuit if they gave too much information, while others argued that integrity demanded full disclosure of the truth.

The board consulted with a Christian attorney, who advised them to keep public communication to a minimum. From his perspective, the church should do everything possible to minimize risk to the organization and should just release Ted without any public statement. However, a number of elders, including Peter and Chip, argued that the church must balance managing risk with communicating truthfully about the situation. The congregation deserved communication that was honest while not disparaging of Ted.

Another concern was the basketball program. Was it a ministry of Lighthouse Church or only of Ted? Ted had incorporated the ministry as a nonprofit organization under the church's tax-exempt umbrella. He had received additional income from the ministry for private coaching, while the programs used Lighthouse's facilities at no cost.

In addition, Ted had received a significant amount of money from Lighthouse when he and his family first relocated to the area to assist with the down payment on a home. Those on the board of elders thought it had been communicated clearly that this was a loan with regular expected payments. Over time, however, Ted had stopped making payments and began to talk of the money as a gift from the church.

After lengthy discussion, the board agreed on a three-part course of action, all of which were approved by Lighthouse's legal counsel:

1. A separation agreement and release of employment to be delivered to Ted. This agreement would provide for salary through date of termination, two and a half months of severance payment, and financial provision for up to twelve sessions of professional counseling each for Ted and his family within six months after termination. Lighthouse would also forgive the housing assistance loan but would retain the fees received for basketball programs, along with all basketball equipment purchased by the church. Ted would no longer be allowed to use church facilities or equipment for Park Pride.

2. A statement to be read to the congregation at the conclusion of each of the two upcoming Sunday worship services. This statement would announce that the board had voted to dismiss Ted for violation of the church's code of ethics concerning pastors and of church policy concerning electronic communications, both of which were in direct reference to the church staff handbook. The statement also noted that the board deeply regretted having to take this action and was committed to treating Ted and his family fairly, compassionately, and generously. In addition, although they knew there would be many questions, the board would not be able to provide further detail.

3. A statement to be emailed to all families involved with Park Pride. This statement would announce Ted's dismissal for violation of policy and invite parents to a meeting to address the future of the basketball ministry.

Per the church's bylaws, written notice was given of the upcoming congregational meeting; when the day came, the church was packed. During the service, Peter preached about sin in the camp from Joshua 7, a passage which had been scheduled months earlier. The elders chair read the prepared statement at the end of each service. The board then sent the same statement via email to the congregation and to the Park Pride community.

At the Park Pride meeting the following week, the elders chair reread the statement, adding that Ted had not been charged with any crime and that there was no indication of impropriety within Park Pride. However, Ted was no longer allowed in the church building and would not be able to continue leading the ministry on church property.

Over the next few weeks, Ted searched for a new site for the basketball program, but he was unable to find a long-term solution, so the ministry ended a few months after his dismissal from Lighthouse. Ted also needed to find another job. Within six months, he had been hired by a church about seventy-five miles from Lighthouse.

During that time, Chip opened Ted's former church laptop computer to prepare it for use by another staff member. He discovered that Ted had not logged out of any of the websites in his browser and had not changed the passwords. Chip found continued activity on adult websites, along with an updated photos file that included dozens of photos of teenaged girls, including some from Lighthouse and from Park Pride. The photos appeared to have been copied and pasted from the girls' social-media sites and zoomed in or cropped to highlight body parts including chests, buttocks, and legs.

Chip reported his new discoveries to Peter and to the elders chair, and the three of them quickly decided to turn the laptop over to the sheriff's department, requesting a search into whether Ted had committed any criminal activity. After a thorough search, the sheriff's department contacted Ted to notify him that his former work computer had been submitted for search and that the activity discovered came dangerously close to criminal categorization, although no charges would be filed.

Ted was released from his new church six months after beginning employment, ostensibly because of budget cuts. After another year searching for employment, he was hired as senior pastor at a small church twenty minutes from Lighthouse. To Chip and Peter's knowledge, neither of the two subsequent churches called anyone at Lighthouse to check references before hiring Ted.

Approximately one year after Ted began working at the small church, Peter's college-aged son received a text from a female friend at Lighthouse, who had discovered Ted's photo and profile on a popular but sometimes risqué dating app. Ted's profile description referred to suggestive and sadistic sexual behaviors with potential partners. Peter's son found that Ted had an active profile on the app, with very recent activity.

Upon learning this, Peter called the denominational superintendent over Ted's church, who gave Peter the contact information for the church's elders chair, because the denomination respected local church autonomy in staff matters. In his phone conversation with the elders chair, Peter summarized the public facts of Ted's history and reported the latest discovery on the dating app. The elder was surprised by this information and apologetic for not doing additional research during the pastoral search process.

As of this writing five years later, Ted remains in his position.

NOW WHAT?

1. How do you feel now that you've read the entire case and know how it ended?

2. Would you have acted similarly?

3. How could a different result have been achieved?

4. What actions can you, your fellow leaders, and your organization take to prepare for—and perhaps avoid, mitigate, or replicate—this particular situation or outcome?

Recommended Resources

Church Law and Tax website, www.churchlawandtax.com.

Henderson, Daniel. *Glorious Finish: Keeping Your Eye on the Prize of Eternity in a Time of Pastoral Failings.* Chicago: Moody, 2020.

McIntosh, Gary L., and Samuel D. Rima. *Overcoming the Dark Side of Leadership: How to Become an Effective Leader by Confronting Potential Failures.* Grand Rapids: Baker, 2007.

12 | HOW WIDE THE DIVIDES

While most case studies are written in third person, objectively telling the facts of the case, in reality leaders often learn of a situation through personal conversations. This puts a human face, emotions, and a backstory—as well as a more subjective telling—to a case in a way that a third-person description cannot. In that vein, here is Selena's story:

"I grew up in the Southwest with very strong roots, part of a large Hispanic family. My grandparents lived next door to us, and we lived next door to my aunt and uncle, the whole nine yards. I learned Spanish and English simultaneously in our home, but the Spanish language and culture were by far our staple.

"When I was seventeen years old, I received a full scholarship to study music education. I played piano and sang. Music was a huge part of my life. One day I was leading worship at a church service, and I felt the Lord say, 'Stop singing.' And I thought, 'What's that?' It was a new experience for me. But it was a persistent voice, not audible but in my spirit, a voice that said, 'I want you to sing for those who can't hear you. You will lead them into my presence, into my Word.' I had no idea what this message meant.

"At the time, I thought, *Okay, well, maybe I'll take one sign-language class. I'm not giving up everything; like, that's crazy. I'm not just going to stop everything that I've been working on and give up a scholarship. I'm not going to pay for school.*

"I started to slowly transition: one class, one thing at a time. I thought, *Well, Lord, if you really want me to do this, I'll take one class at a time, but I'm not leaving everything.* And then one of my professors said they wanted to recommend me to apply to the interpreter program at my university. Every year, 1,600 people apply and only sixteen are accepted. At that time, I was just in the beginner ASL [American Sign Language] class. But I applied, and I got in the program.

"Shortly after that, my brother told me he found a school in Minnesota and that we should go because it had a program in theology in American Sign Language. And I explained I had already told the Lord I was not going all-in on this. I was only willing to do some little pieces. But I kept having a nagging feeling that I should go. It was the worst experience of my life. I got there, and they forgot to pick us up from the airport. I got to my room late, and nobody had a key to get us into the school. My host wasn't there because her grandmother passed away the night before.

"I started walking around to find my brother, and I heard music, and my heart was just a wreck at that point. It was 11:00 o'clock at night, and I walked into the chapel, where they were having a praise gathering. I walked in and had that same tugging on my heart. God said, 'This is where you're supposed to be,' and I said, 'I'm not moving here.'

"I went back home, but I was still a wreck. A week before school started, I finally told the Lord, 'Okay, I'm all in; I can't take it anymore.' I packed a suitcase and ended up in Minnesota for the next three years. I loved every second of it. God was opening up my heart and mind to the needs of Deaf people around the world and teaching me to have capacity to serve alongside them.

"From there, I was hired as an administrative assistant and language liaison for a national ministry. I was soon promoted to communications manager, then VP of communications, director of advocacy, chief advocacy officer, and then to CEO in early 2020.

"I felt the Lord had called me to be a bridge to ensure that Deaf and hearing people have unhindered access to each other. But I'm a hearing person, and nearly everyone in our office is Deaf. Communication with our team is all in American Sign Language. So every day I need to take off my 'hearing hat' and think about how I communicate—not just with ASL in the office but our methods with constituents. There has been no roadmap for connecting sign languages to written donors, written constituents, written business partners.

"There are racial aspects, gender aspects, and age aspects to this as well. I'm Hispanic. I'm a woman. I'm young. I had just turned twenty-four when I started here and was in my early thirties when I became CEO. I gather monthly with a group of CEOs who are in the same type of ministry, and they are predominantly white, male, and older. How do I have unity and equality and oneness with a male leader who is in his sixties? People have told me they wouldn't give to our organization because I sounded too young.

"When I first started in an executive capacity at our ministry, I was asked to lead our building project. I was super excited. I wanted us to think about depth, space, and lighting. I had a vision for what it could look like. We had a limited budget, but I found a great used-furniture place where we could get items ten cents on the dollar. I was really excited to give a report to the staff. I went into this meeting and signed, 'Guys, this is awesome. We're going to get this used furniture.' And the tone of the room completely changed.

"I thought, *Why is everybody so upset? Do people have a problem with used furniture?* I grew up with secondhand stores, but I didn't know why that would be a problem. I left that meeting not understanding why I didn't get any feedback or why the body language had shifted.

"I felt like people were writing me off, so I finally went to one of the other leaders and asked why everyone was being so standoffish about this project. And he shared with me, 'I didn't appreciate the fact that you told me you were going to get furniture that was your preference.' I asked what he meant, and he said, 'Well, you signed us "used," which meant that you were just going with the furniture that you liked.'

"I thought I signed 'used,' but the sign I chose actually meant 'used to'—as in, what I was used to, my preferences—instead of 'secondhand,' which is a completely different sign, a completely different concept.

"That set the tone for the entire team as to how we would work together moving forward. For those Deaf individuals, it meant, 'Here's another hearing person who thinks it's about them, not us. They don't see me and my value as a Deaf person. They want to do things their way. It's Deaf people being oppressed, yet again. I don't have a voice.' All that trauma flooded through our culture in that one meeting. Meeting after meeting after meeting, it didn't matter that I corrected myself and apologized over and over again. The damage was done.

"It took three years of trying to lead that team after that building project. The repercussions continued when I became CEO. All the years of holding on to that trauma: I'm a hearing person, I'm not connected to Deaf people, and now I've been asked to lead a Deaf organization where 80 percent of our team is Deaf. I had to communicate with them not in my native language, and they were not my native people group.

"My first day as CEO, a majority of our Deaf staff wrote a petition to have me removed and to pick someone else. By that time I had been there almost seven years.

"One week later, I found out the building we were in was not ADA [American Disabilities Act] compliant, so I couldn't have Deaf staff work there because it wasn't safe if there was an emergency. We went from people wanting me removed, to me telling them we couldn't have them in our building. Our donations went down 50 percent, and all of the Deaf staff pointed at me as the one person who was making all of this happen to them. I didn't know what could be done to close the gaps."

QUESTIONS FOR REFLECTION

1. With the information you've been given, how would you summarize the problem(s) in this case?

2. Who are the main characters and what are their roles in this situation?

3. What assumptions and values do you hear voiced by these characters?

4. What other information do you wish you had about this situation?

5. What seem to be the technical challenges involved in this case?

6. What are the adaptive challenges, and what type of adaptive challenges are they?

7. What risks and opportunities do you see in this case?

8. What biblical and theological principles should be considered in this case?

9. What are your suggested next steps for the parties involved?

10. What longer-term considerations might impact short-term decisions?

11. What work should be given "back to the people" here? To whom, and how?

12. What assumptions and values guide your recommended course of action?

13. What responses did you notice within yourself as you read this case?

14. Do you think anything could have been done differently, either individually or organizationally, to avoid this situation? If so, what?

15. Might this case be different if:

    a) Selena had fewer cultural differences within her leadership context? For example, if she were older, white, Deaf, and/or male?

    b) She had not experienced such a strong and clear sense of calling to ministry to the Deaf community?

    c) You were reading it as a third-person objective account, instead of through Selena's perspective?

16. Issues to consider:

a) What are the biblical and theological values and principles that should guide discussion and actions regarding differences such as ethnicity, culture, gender, and age?

b) How should a leader's personal calling and story fit into their role and to their relationship with an organization, and vice-versa?

c) What principles and practices can leaders use to build unity among diverse groups?

Commentary

Selena thought her job was to bridge the divide from the Deaf community to the hearing community and to make the hearing community aware of the needs of Deaf people in her organization's area of ministry. However, as she discovered, there were multiple cultural divides: as a hearing person, leading within an organization of Deaf people and Deaf culture; as a young executive, working with other CEOs several times her age; as a woman, interacting with predominantly male counterparts; and as a Hispanic minority, leading in a white culture. Each of these started out as general challenges, but an inadvertent miscommunication in this climate of general challenge led to an acute problem with the possibility of more problems down the road.

Selena's passion, clear sense of calling, and good intentions have not been enough to mitigate these gaps. To move forward, she will need to work carefully and slowly to build and rebuild trust to bridge these many divides while also dealing with an unpredictable external reality brought on by a global pandemic.

| ADDITIONAL QUESTIONS |

1. Has your initial diagnosis of this situation changed? If so, how and why?

2. Which character(s) do you find yourself empathizing with?

3. Do you need to revise or address any of your assumptions?

Epilogue

SELENA'S STORY CONTINUES:

"I had no roadmap to know how to fill the cultural gaps. I couldn't fix it quickly, and I had no idea how much time it was going to take.

"Ten months after I became CEO, the staff completely revolted. There was toxicity, dysfunction, anger, and private meetings. There were phone calls to the board sharing untruths: that my husband was abusing me, that I was spiritually gaslighting people. I wondered, *Lord, when and where did this start? What could I have done to close the gaps so I wouldn't have to experience this moment?*

"Come November of that year, despite every attempt to bring clarity and resolution and consistency to the team, trauma healing for the staff, providing free counseling, I hadn't experienced a single win. I said, 'We are at a point where there are some things internally that need to be changed or removed for us to move forward. If this continues, we won't make it, and I won't make it. . . . I can't continue in this way with the amount of tension, lack of trust, and dysfunction, so we need to just pause and really consider what the organization is going to keep—including me, I'm putting myself on the table—and what we are not going to keep to ensure we move to a healthy step in the very near future.'

"Our board never wavered in their support of me. Once I called for that, they said okay, and within two weeks, they shared with the entire staff that starting January 1, everyone would be on a six-week respite, during which the board would conduct an intense audit of all positions, staff, and finances. After that, they would let everyone know who would be staying and who would not.

"Some of the biggest allies we had were our board and some of our strategic partners in our alliance. We are part of a collective impact alliance of eleven Bible-translation-focused agencies and five resourcing partners who have committed to likeminded goals. We meet monthly as CEOs and funding partners to talk about our collective goals while maintaining our own organizational identities to see our collective impact thrive.

"In that space, I was inundated by support from a body of people with similar goals who had only the best interests for me and our organization at heart. Some of them would send me encouraging text messages weekly. In addition to that, we had a very supportive board—a listening board, a board that was committed to taking action when action was appropriately needed.

"In December and January, I did an entire summary of the organization, of recommendations, of project statuses. The board brought in an interim leadership team comprised of a variety of executive leaders from the alliance, including an interim COO from another organization to serve two to three months.

"For me, those six weeks included a crazy amount of work. Someone still had to guide details regarding the building, payroll, and projects. I had to support the interim leadership team, and they needed information about the organization. A lot was still in motion while they were making high-level strategic decisions. It was exhausting for me and for my family. But the process brought clarity about what was necessary to put the organization in a better spot.

"When I came to the organization, we had sixty to eighty staff at our headquarters. When I became CEO, I shared with the board a recommendation to become more efficient. I felt that more dollars needed to hit the field. We were a heavy, US-centric organization when our mission was to reach the nations and to provide opportunities in other nations. My goal was to adjust the team to promote Deaf people elsewhere rather than building a Deaf empire within the US.

"So after I became CEO, we reduced the onsite staff to half, around thirty people. Then, after the respite, the board called back fifteen staff members, including me. We moved back in as an extremely healthy team, thankful for the decisions the board made.

"But I didn't fully recover right away. Shortly after coming back, I went on what felt like an apology tour. After letting people go—with so much change and so much fallout from that change—partnerships were harder. Some of our former employees went to work at Deaf partnering agencies. We had to work through reconciliation and acceptance of change and of one another.

"One of the things we recognized was that trust, loyalty, and commitment are harder to train. We started there: How can we build a healthy culture of people who are for each other? We tell each other every day, 'We're not perfect; we haven't figured everything out.' But our commitment to learning, to growing, to failing forward has made the most significant changes. We also focused on consistency, on chasing after our mission with excellence.

"I regularly share our vision statement with my team. There

are a lot of words in it, but the word that keeps me going is *opportunity*. The Lord keeps providing avenues for us to come up with creative solutions to see needs met. When I come to work, I see that opportunity, and I want to give other people opportunities. It comes back to the initial idea that Jesus has given us an opportunity to know him, to become like him, to have eternity with him. Because we're centered around opportunity, around solutions, that has helped us navigate more difficult things like PTSD among staff, lack of training, lack of answers to questions, and more.

"I can't speak enough to how faithful the Lord has been through this. Before I became CEO, we were in a predicament with our finances. We were growing an empire but not having impact and output with dollars placed missionally. Now, not even three years later, we have almost tripled in revenue. We can't start projects as quickly as investors want us to move. We have experienced an outpouring of generosity beyond measure.

"Getting here was hard, and it has been brutal, but along the way people came alongside me. The hope I see through it is an effort to bridge cultures: racial differences, communication differences, leadership and age differences. I've witnessed these godly leaders say, 'This is too big for any one of us. I don't know how to connect to Deaf people, but I want to try. I don't have the roadmap, but I believe that unity will get us there.'"

Now What?

1. How do you feel now that you've read the entire case and know how it ended?

2. Would you have acted similarly?

3. How could a different result have been achieved?

4. What actions can you, your fellow leaders, and your organization take to prepare for—and perhaps avoid, mitigate, or replicate—this particular situation or outcome?

Recommended Resources

Grenny, Joseph, Kerry Patterson, Ron McMillan, Al Switzler, and Emily Gregory. *Crucial Conversations: Tools for Talking When Stakes Are High.* 3rd ed. New York: McGraw Hill, 2022.

Lingenfelter, Sherwood. *Leading Cross-Culturally: Covenant Relationships for Effective Christian Leadership.* Grand Rapids: Baker Academic, 2008.

Shaw, Haydn. *Sticking Points: How to Get Five Generations Working Together in the Twelve Places They Come Apart.* Carol Stream, IL: Tyndale Momentum, 2020.

13 | LETTER VERSUS SPIRIT

Juliet and Santiago began attending Hope Fellowship after they discovered they were pregnant and that the baby, their second, would have significant birth defects. The congregation welcomed the young couple and prayed with them as they shared their fears about the difficulties this child would have. The congregation's encouragement helped assure them abortion was not the only option for such a pregnancy, and they decided Juliet would carry the baby to full term.

Even though Juliet and Santiago were not married, the congregation warmly welcomed and supported the couple. "We don't pull back when people are in need," said the pastor. "We want to be where Jesus would be—and that's walking alongside people even in messy situations."

When Juliet and Santiago expressed their deep appreciation for the congregation's support, the leaders of Hope Fellowship felt affirmed. They had been seeking ways to reach out to the Spanish-speaking community near the church.

When little Javier was born with misshapen legs and a compromised immune system, the congregation prayed him through the treatments and surgeries and brought meals and baby outfits to the family and toys for older brother Pedro.

A year later, Juliet had committed her life to Christ and was in a women's Bible study, eager to grow in her faith. Santiago, however, did not find close connections at church, and while he was supportive of Juliet's church involvement, his attendance was sporadic.

Then Juliet, in response to a sermon on the value of church membership, applied to become a member at Hope Fellowship. When she met with the elders to share her testimony, she happily told them about accepting Christ and being discipled by the women in the church to be a faithful mom to Pedro and Javier.

One of the elders asked Juliet if she and Santiago ever talked about getting married. "Oh, I would love to get married," she said. "But Santiago says we can't afford it. I'm on Medicaid, and if we got married, his insurance premiums would more than triple. Javier continues to need treatments and medical supplies. We're barely making it on Santiago's paycheck as it is. Someday we can get married, but Santiago says there's no way right now."

The interview ended with the elders thanking Juliet for her testimony and praying for her. They said they'd be back in touch regarding the membership process.

As they debriefed afterward, the elders realized they weren't in agreement about whether to approve Juliet for membership. Those not in support of Juliet's application for membership emphasized that having sex without being married means the couple was living in an ongoing sinful relationship and that the church could not endorse open, ongoing sin as acceptable for members. Endorsing her as a church member while she was living in sin would be a bad example and an even worse precedent. Even if Juliet and Santiago were to marry, she would be "unequally yoked" according to their understanding of 2 Corinthians 6:14: "Do not be yoked together with unbelievers. For what do righteousness and wickedness have in common? Or what fellowship can light have with darkness?" In light of this passage, Juliet would need to separate from Santiago if she were to become a member of the church.

Others, however, wanted to approve Juliet for membership. They emphasized that Juliet was a believer, growing in her faith. No one is without sin, they pointed out, and while her relationship with Santiago may have started out as sin, Juliet was now being faithful to her children and to their father. She was being as obedient to Jesus as she could be. She wanted to get married but couldn't if Santiago would not consent. And she was right not to make her children fatherless by leaving Santiago. The spirit of 1 Corinthians 7:13–17 should apply:

> And if a woman has a husband who is not a believer and he is willing to live with her, she must not divorce him. For the unbelieving husband has been sanctified through his wife, and the unbelieving wife has been sanctified through her believing husband. Otherwise your children would be unclean, but as it is, they are holy.
>
> But if an unbeliever leaves, let it be so. The brother or the sister is not bound in such circumstances; God has called us to live in peace. How do you know, wife, whether you will save your husband? Or, how do you know, husband, whether you will save your wife?
>
> Nevertheless, each person should live as a believer in whatever situation the Lord has assigned to them, just as God has called them. This is the rule I lay down in all the churches.

The elders were unified in their desire to obey Scripture, but in this case, it seemed that there was biblical support for both perspectives.

QUESTIONS FOR REFLECTION

1. With the information you've been given, how would you summarize the problem(s) in this case?

2. Who are the main characters and what are their roles in this situation?

3. What assumptions and values do you hear voiced by these characters?

4. What other information do you wish you had about this situation?

5. What seem to be the technical challenges involved in this case?

6. What are the adaptive challenges, and what type of adaptive challenges are they?

7. What risks and opportunities do you see in this case?

8. What biblical and theological principles should be considered in this case?

9. What are your suggested next steps for the parties involved?

10. What longer-term considerations might impact short-term decisions?

11. What work should be given "back to the people" here? To whom, and how?

12. What assumptions and values guide your recommended course of action?

13. What responses did you notice within yourself as you read this case?

14. Do you think anything could have been done differently, either individually or organizationally, to avoid this situation? If so, what?

15. Might this case be different if:

    a) Santiago were a believer?

    b) The couple did not have children?

    c) Juliet wanted to serve as a volunteer, which did not depend on church membership?

16. Issues to consider:

    a) What does it look like to maintain biblical integrity for a congregation while caring personally and pastorally for a congregant? What are the risks for prioritizing one concern over the other?

    b) How would you define grace? What does it entail institutionally and interpersonally?

    c) What is your view of church membership? Who can become a member and what privileges and responsibilities come with it?

Commentary

As with many adaptive leadership challenges, the decision facing the elders involves not only the matter of Juliet's membership. As those against her acceptance pointed out, this decision would set a precedent for how to deal with similar situations in the future. In addition, the question was based on two different sets of values for interpreting and applying Scripture. Is there a Hope Fellowship "way" for these types of questions—not just of decision but of biblical interpretation—that has already been determined? If not, should there be, and who should decide? If not, how will future disagreements be arbitrated? What may seem like a no-brainer decision to some (in either direction) has more nuances and implications than may be initially visible.

| ADDITIONAL QUESTIONS |

1. Has your initial diagnosis of this situation changed? If so, how and why?

2. Which character(s) do you find yourself empathizing with?

3. Do you need to revise or address any of your assumptions?

Epilogue

The elders of Hope Fellowship were not able to come to a decision during the meeting, so they asked one of the elders, Miles Curry, to meet with Santiago to see whether he would consider putting his faith in Christ. Over breakfast, Santiago noted that he was open to marriage, but he had looked into the financial ramifications, and his health insurance premiums would triple if he added Juliet and the children to his plan. Santiago worked as a warehouse laborer and did not feel he could meet the additional expense. Miles asked Santiago, if the church were willing to pick up the difference in premium expenses for a year, would that be enough provision that Santiago could marry Juliet in faith and trust that God would take care of the family after that? Santiago said no.

Miles then inquired about Santiago's relationship with Christ. "Are you willing to trust Jesus, to get to the same place that Juliet is?" Santiago acknowledged that he was open to it and thinking about it. He understood the significance of the decision and was not ready to make a commitment to Christ. Miles reassured Santiago that he respected Santiago's choice and that the church cared for him, Juliet, and their children. The question of Juliet's membership was paused while the elders hoped God would bring some change in the situation.

Six weeks later, Juliet called Miles. "I need you to talk to Santiago," she said. Santiago had been arrested for his second charge of driving while intoxicated and was being held at the jail. However, Santiago was embarrassed and ashamed and would not give Miles or anyone else permission to visit him in jail. Miles told Juliet to convey that he would love to talk to Santiago if he ever agreed to that.

Three weeks later after he had been released from jail, Santiago called Miles. "We need to get together so I can tell you what happened," Santiago said.

Over another breakfast, Santiago related his story. "I was in the county jail, and it was awful. You can see and hear guys in other cells, but I was completely isolated. The jail took my phone, and there was nothing to do. I saw another guy had some books, so I asked if I could borrow one. He first said no, but then I asked if he could spare one that he wasn't reading, and he finally said yes. He slid a book to me. I had no idea what it was about, but it was called *The Purpose Driven Life*. It was missing the first thirty-eight pages, but I picked it up and started reading it. That book was describing me! It said you have to live for something bigger than yourself, that your life has purpose, and it's not all about you. I had just five small pieces of paper and a stub of a pencil, but I took notes and filled all of the paper front and back about what God said about my life."

"It sounds like God was speaking to you about your life,"

Miles observed. "Is that enough to convince you to invite Jesus into your life?"

"Yes, I think that's the next step!" Santiago replied.

The two men prayed together as Santiago asked Jesus to be the Lord of his life. Miles hugged Santiago. "This is a big moment!" he said. "You've got to tell Juliet, Pedro, and Javier that God spoke to you in jail through this book."

When Santiago reported what had happened, Juliet was thrilled, as were the elders of Hope Fellowship. Juliet requested that she and Santiago be baptized at the same time, which was her dream come true. Miles and his wife were afforded the honor of baptizing the couple. But thirty minutes before the service, Santiago walked up to Miles. "We've got a problem," he announced. "My ankle monitor isn't supposed to be submerged in water." Miles quickly fashioned a protective wrap out of a trash bag and duct tape. When Miles submerged Santiago, his balloon-wrapped ankle popped above the water, much to the amusement of the congregation who had gathered to support the family.

A few weeks later, Miles sought out Santiago again. "Santiago, you've made a big decision to follow Christ" he said. "Are you willing to trust Jesus with making your kids legal and marrying their mother?"

"Yeah, we can do that," Santiago agreed. "Will you do the service?"

Several weeks later, Miles officiated Santiago and Juliet's wedding at a beautiful arboretum in front of thirty-five friends and relatives. Miles signed the marriage certificate and instructed Juliet to take it to the county courthouse for registration.

A week later, Miles saw Juliet at church and asked whether she had submitted it to the courthouse. "No, we're married in the sight of God," Juliet said. "We don't need to do it for the state. The kids and I would lose our public health insurance."

Meanwhile, the elders agreed to welcome Juliet to church membership. However, Santiago decided he did not need to be part of the congregation. The church continued to care for Juliet and her children, providing various material needs for the family. Several years later, the family of four moved out of state.

NOW WHAT?

1. How do you feel now that you've read the entire case and know how it ended?

2. Would you have acted similarly?

3. How could a different result have been achieved?

4. What actions can you, your fellow leaders, and your organization take to prepare for—and perhaps avoid, mitigate, or replicate—this particular situation or outcome?

Recommended Resources

Baker, Mark D. *Centered-Set Church: Discipleship and Community without Judgmentalism.* Downers Grove, IL: IVP Academic, 2022.

Kimble, Jeremy M. *Forty Questions about Church Membership and Discipline.* Forty Questions. Grand Rapids: Kregel Academic, 2017.

Leeman, Jonathan. *Church Membership: How the World Knows Who Represents Jesus.* 9Marks: Building Healthy Churches. Wheaton, IL: Crossway, 2012.

COMPASSION, INTERNATIONAL

Corey Jenkins was the pastor of Calvary Church, a midsized congregation located in a first-ring suburb of a large city. After generations of turnover, this aging suburb was now home to an Indian immigrant community, which Corey and the Calvary congregation felt called to welcome and serve. Calvary Church financially supported several missionaries to India and had sponsored several short-term missions trips there. Corey had also taken several trips to that poverty-stricken region of the world, which spurred his heart for the Indian people and the church's ministry to the immigrant community.

Two years ago, a Christian immigrant family from India had joined Calvary Church and proceeded to bring numerous visitors from the Indian subcontinent with them. Some stayed; others didn't. Eight months ago, a pregnant woman in her thirties named Indira and her two young children visited with the Christian family and became regular attenders. Indira claimed to be a believer, and while her Christian walk was inconsistent, Corey had no reason to doubt her profession of faith.

When Corey first met Indira, Indira told him that her husband, Rajan, who was the visa holder for the family, had recently gone back to India because of job-related matters, but that subsequent problems with the Indian government and with American immigration services seemed to be making it impossible for him to return. Meanwhile, Indira was into the third term of her pregnancy and had virtually no resources left to live on or to provide for her children.

Because of his and the church's special interest in India, Corey felt that God was leading him to go the extra mile to help Indira and her family. God also seemed to be providing for the family because a young couple in the church, Jake and Kathy Dunbar, volunteered to house the family in their spacious home while Indira tried to figure out her husband's situation and to investigate options for reuniting the family.

As the weeks passed, however, it seemed to Jake and Kathy that Indira was no longer trying very hard to be reunited with her husband. Rajan was a Christian too, and a leader in an Indian Christian parachurch organization. But stories about his irresponsibility with money and his leaving the family for long stretches at a time, supposedly because of his work but even when they all lived together in India, surfaced. Indira admitted that he had not been sexually unfaithful to her nor had subjected her to violence, but he often refused to take even basic steps to provide for her. Indira's attempts to contact Rajan were unsuccessful, as emails and phone calls were not returned. Contacting Rajan's Indian employer led to conflicting and confusing information about his whereabouts and about what that organization knew about his situation. But at least one high-level executive sounded genuinely shocked to learn that Rajan had returned to India without his family.

Eventually, Jake and Kathy's patience wore thin. They explained to Indira that she could not stay with them indefinitely. If it did not appear that Rajan was going to come back to the United States, then she needed to begin planning to take her family back home after the new baby was born and mother and new child had a reasonable amount of time to prepare. But Indira took no further steps. Soon she had a new, healthy baby boy to look after as well.

Still feeling that Indira was more of the victim in this situation, Corey arranged for a Christian halfway house in town to take Indira and her three children so Jake and Kathy wouldn't be spending any more of their money and time on the family. Corey had long ago exhausted the church's deacons fund in helping to provide for Indira and her children. Fortunately, the missions budget had some extra money available, and because the family was from overseas, the congregation seemed to think it was acceptable—some even thought it obligatory—to use these funds to help them. The chair of the missions committee acquiesced but pointed out that this need didn't really have anything more to do with missions than other ministries, such as the women's or children's ministries.

More time passed, and Corey felt led to take more action by trying to raise the money needed—approximately $4,500—to put the family of four on a plane and send them back to India to be reunited with Rajan. Once the funds were raised, Indira seemed to agree, albeit somewhat reluctantly, that this was the right thing to do. So Corey purchased the plane tickets for her. However, Indira then announced that she couldn't find the passports for the two children and that the baby never had a passport in the first place. Corey contacted the relevant offices in the United States and in India and learned that the situation could be rectified for another $750. Frustrated but now wanting to be rid of what had become more of a problem than anticipated, Corey worked to raise additional money.

Then a phone call came from Rajan's employer in India. Rajan had told his employer that it was the two countries' governments that were preventing the family from being reunited in the United States, and that Indira and the children would have to fly home. The company gave him $2,000 toward the travel expenses. But now the $2,000 had disappeared; apparently Rajan had spent it on something else. Yet Rajan continued to insist that his family must return, even while showing no signs of any willingness to provide for them upon their arrival.

Corey's inquiries with an immigration services representative made it clear that if Indira and her children stayed in the US, they would be illegal immigrants, subject to potential deportation at any time. But if Corey carried through with the plan to send them home with the nonrefundable airplane tickets he had purchased (along with new passports, visas, and other incidental travel expenses), there was no guarantee that Rajan would be there to welcome them, much less provide for them. Moreover, the Indian welfare system would not be able to adequately provide for Indira and her children.

Questions for Reflection

1. With the information you've been given, how would you summarize the problem(s) in this case?

2. Who are the main characters and what are their roles in this situation?

3. What assumptions and values do you hear voiced by these characters?

4. What other information do you wish you had about this situation?

5. What seem to be the technical challenges involved in this case?

6. What are the adaptive challenges, and what type of adaptive challenges are they?

7. What risks and opportunities do you see in this case?

8. What biblical and theological principles should be considered in this case?

9. What are your suggested next steps for the parties involved?

10. What longer-term considerations might impact short-term decisions?

11. What work should be given "back to the people" here? To whom, and how?

12. What assumptions and values guide your recommended course of action?

13. What responses did you notice within yourself as you read this case?

14. Do you think anything could have been done differently, either individually or organizationally, to avoid this situation? If so, what?

15. Might this case be different if:

    a) Rajan communicated some willingness to care for his wife and children or had a record of responsible and honest behavior?

    b) Indira and her children would not be illegal immigrants if they stayed in the US?

    c) Indira did not claim to be a Christian?

    d) Indira did not have young children?

16. Issues to consider:

   a) What are the limits to a church or ministry helping an individual or a family in need? What and who determines those limits?

   b) What is the responsibility of a church toward immigrants and refugees vis-a-vis local, state, or national government regulations?

   c) How much weight should precedent—either following it or setting it—be given in decisions regarding care, recognition, financial support, and/or even reappropriation of designated funds?

Commentary

For Corey, what seemed at first to be an easy decision to assist Indira and her children in the short term has mushroomed into a costly, potentially long-term burden with no easy solution. Indira does not have the resources to care for her children on her own. And with Rajan back in India, she and her children are living in the US as illegal immigrants. It could be very expensive to help Indira get established legally and in suitable housing and employment in the United States—if she even wants that.

Meanwhile, Calvary Church presumably has a limit to what it can provide financially. To this point, Corey has used church budget money and raised funds as needed, thinking that each next expenditure would be the last. There already seems to be some internal questioning about using funds not designated for this purpose. But how do you put a price or an expense limit on the well-being of a mother and her children?

Then there is the issue of the church's witness. How will

Indira, Rajan, their children, the church, and the Indian congregants and surrounding community view Calvary Church, and by extension Jesus Christ, depending on what Corey and the congregation decide to do about Indira and her family? Corey and Calvary's leadership must weigh the options and their associated costs—not all of them immediate or financial—and decide which are worth bearing for both the short and long term.

Additional Questions

1. Has your initial diagnosis of this situation changed? If so, how and why?

2. Which character(s) do you find yourself empathizing with?

3. Do you need to revise or address any of your assumptions?

Epilogue

Corey felt that he could not leave Indira and her children to deal with the situation entirely on their own. Yet he also realized that he needed more input from others in the church regarding a viable solution beyond reactionary, short-term funding.

In consultation with the chair of the missions committee, the church treasurer, and several elders, it was decided that Indira needed to be made aware of the seriousness of the illegal immigration concerns and the impact that deportation could have on her family. In his conversation with her, Corey explained that Jake and Kathy could house Indira and her children for several more months, until everyone had visas and the newborn was old enough to travel. The church could also cover the costs for the family to travel back to India but could not provide financially beyond those arrangements. This conversation helped Indira realize that she could not just coast indefinitely without a plan. She reached out to Rajan more earnestly.

Meanwhile, Calvary Church sent a short-term missions team to India that had been planned months ago for unrelated purposes. While there the team, including the missions committee chair, tracked Rajan down and leveled with him that it was his responsibility to welcome the family back, live with them in compassion and consideration, and provide for them. Rajan was utterly shocked that Americans would show up on his doorstep and assured them he would fulfill his obligation, although the team wasn't sure whether his commitment was genuine.

Nevertheless, a few months after the short-term trip and about six months after Indira's baby had been born, Calvary Church sent the family home to India, where they moved back in with Rajan. Corey and the congregation soon lost touch with them and never learned how things went over time, including whether the family remained together.

Corey and the leadership of Calvary Church used the situation with Indira and her children as an impetus to evaluate and clarify its budget policies for missions, benevolence, and immigrant ministries.

NOW WHAT?

1. How do you feel now that you've read the entire case and know how it ended?

2. Would you have acted similarly?

3. How could a different result have been achieved?

4. What actions can you, your fellow leaders, and your
   organization take to prepare for—and perhaps avoid,
   mitigate, or replicate—this particular situation or outcome?

Recommended Resources

Annan, Kent. *You Welcomed Me: Loving Refugees and Immigrants
because God First Loved Us.* Downers Grove, IL: InterVarsity
Press, 2018.

Hoover, Sharon R. *Mapping Church Missions: A Compass for
Ministry Strategy.* Downers Grove, IL: InterVarsity Press,
2018.

Mandes, Alejandro. *Embracing the New Samaria: Opening Our Eyes
to Our Multiethnic Future.* Colorado Springs, CO: NavPress,
2021.

CONFLICTING
CONCLUSIONS

Lambert Theological School (LTS) is a small ministry-training
school in the American central Midwest. Its mission is to provide
graduate-level education for ministry leaders within and beyond
its founding denomination, the Evangelical Church of Christ
(ECoC). The ECoC is a small Protestant denomination, its 350
churches grouped within seven regions around the country but
centered predominantly in the Midwest, particularly in the central (where Lambert is located) and neighboring east-central
regions.

While Lambert is the official school of the ECoC, the
denomination does not control the institution. The ECoC selects
Lambert's board members, but the board of trustees then makes
decisions independent of any other denominational control.

For decades, there had been a belief that LTS needed a formal presence in the east-central region, where the denomination
had been founded and where the ECoC had a large concen-
tration of churches. Approximately twelve years ago, a group
of ECoC pastors and board members from that region began
a more focused push toward that end with broad support from
within both organizations, including the longtime president

of LTS. It seemed that an expansion would benefit all parties, including the ECoC, Lambert, and the churches in the region.

LTS hired a new staff member, Cam Newberg, to spearhead what became known as the Findlay Project, named after a historic figure in the denomination. Newberg soon identified a state government building for sale in a prime location in the region. Thanks to enthusiastic support from area pastors and diligent fundraising efforts, LTS was able to purchase the property, with the ECoC's Home Missions Council and a local bank each providing a portion of the loan for the remaining funding necessary for the purchase.

The intent was to purchase and then transfer the property to a newly formed entity referred to as the Findlay Campus, Inc. The separate entity would then manage the property at arm's length from Lambert Theological School, which would in turn lease space from the Findlay Campus, Inc., board for educational offerings in the neighboring state as "LTS on the Findlay Campus." To do this, LTS also needed approval from the state's higher-learning commission.

While the intent was to quickly transfer the property to the Findlay Campus board of directors, a legal opinion was received identifying the transaction as subject to transfer tax on the assessed value, resulting in tax bill of $690,000 payable on transfer. In light of this unexpected financial burden, the decision was made to retain the property in the Lambert Theological School name pending a reassessment of the property. Despite the lack of transfer, LTS began to take steps to offer courses at the Findlay Campus, as per the intent of the purchase.

The Findlay Campus board of directors remained a legal entity but did not have control of any property. Since LTS continued to hold the property, a staff position was created in the LTS organization, Vice-President of the Findlay Project, to manage the day-to-day operations of the location. Cam Newberg was promoted to this new position.

The property was reassessed six months later, resulting in a reduction in the potential tax resulting from transfer. However, the transfer to Findlay Campus, Inc., was delayed because one of the financing entities, the ECoC Home Missions Council, was concerned about a lack of demonstrated financial history for the Findlay Campus organization.

Meanwhile, LTS determined that it was still best to move toward offering classes at the new campus because the profit from these classes could offset the carrying costs of the property while the transfer was being negotiated. LTS sought approval from state and national accrediting agencies to use the Findlay property as an additional location.

The state and national agencies both responded with initial approval for the additional location. Upon receiving this news, the LTS board of trustees, the Findlay Campus board of directors, and the ECoC executed a memorandum of understanding (MOU) stating that the Findlay Campus corporation would lease the Findlay property from LTS.

One year later, the Home Missions Council transferred the debt for the property to the Findlay Campus corporation board. Once the corporation had demonstrated sufficient history of fiscal responsibility, the property itself was to be transferred. Meanwhile, LTS retained responsibility for the educational operating expenses at the Findlay site. To a casual observer, it seemed that things were going well despite a few speed bumps. A peek behind the curtain, however, revealed no small amount of upheaval.

As the Findlay property situation played out more slowly than anticipated—it was now nearly three years since the initial purchase offer—the president of LTS retired after twenty-seven years and the school began a search for its next president. Meanwhile, the national accrediting board put the institution on probation because the muddied property transfer situation did not meet its accreditation requirements for clear financial processes, institutional planning, and institutional assessment. This meant that LTS's ability to offer programs at the Findlay site was in jeopardy.

In addition, the drawn-out process exposed conflicting values among administrators, staff, board members, and even donors affiliated with each of the entities involved. The former LTS president had wanted to pursue any opportunity that might bring additional income to the school. Some of the LTS board members from the east-central region felt that representation of their region was more important than what might be best for the overall institution. And donors had differing commitments behind their giving: some were committed to LTS, some to the Findlay campus, some to the east-central region, and some to the denomination. When the purchase, transfer, and use of the Findlay property did not proceed as quickly or smoothly as anticipated, constituents began defending their interests instead of unifying around the intended partnership.

The presidential search process was coming to a close, and several finalists had been identified. Only one of them did *not* have a vested interest in the Findlay property issue. After final interviews, the nonaffiliated candidate, Terry Slayton, was selected as the new president of Lambert Theological School, three and a half years after the property search had been initiated.

At Terry's first board meeting as president elect, a board member—a close friend of one of the presidential finalists, also a board member—chastised the group: "You guys hired the wrong guy," he declared in front of Terry as he announced his resignation. Nevertheless, Terry began his first official day on December 1 of that year onsite at the Findlay campus, firmly wanting to make the partnership work.

Five months later, the Home Missions Council determined that sufficient financial history was available for transfer of the property to the control of the Findlay Campus board. The LTS board approved the transfer pending the accreditors' review and removal of probationary status.

However, by this time Terry and others at LTS were wondering whether continued use of the Findlay campus would be wise. While the 160-acre grounds were beautiful, the buildings were old and in desperate need of costly maintenance that had been deferred for years. LTS was still working diligently to emerge from probation, which required additional concentrated effort from staff. Furthermore, the shape of theological higher education was changing with fewer students pursuing residential programs. The Findlay site, purchased on the belief that it would bring more money to the school, was earning less and costing more than anticipated.

Still, the site had strong advocates. The disagreement had already become political; it then became theological.

Those who had been part of the exploration and purchase process and who continued to advocate for the site recalled that the project had been characterized as "the impossible dream." Successful acquisition was evidence of God's mighty work. The LTS board members in favor of the site pointed out that Terry had not been involved when God had brought all the details together and provided the funding for the purchase. Terry's questioning was a sign of a lack of faith not only in the work done by others prior to his arrival at LTS but also in God's provision.

Terry and his staff persisted in their research regarding the Findlay campus and the future of LTS. They felt that the board had a responsibility to practice wise financial stewardship in the best interests of the school. And to Terry, all signs seemed to say that continuing to utilize the Findlay campus, with all its attendant expenses, would not be good stewardship.

By the following spring, Terry was a little more than two years into his tenure as president of LTS. The school had received permission to transfer the Findlay property to the Findlay Campus corporation. LTS could continue to lease classroom space at the Findlay site, which would also be used for other denominational training programs. The next regular LTS board meeting was scheduled for the end of May.

QUESTIONS FOR REFLECTION

1. With the information you've been given, how would you summarize the problem(s) in this case?

2. Who are the main characters and what are their roles in this situation?

3. What assumptions and values do you hear voiced by these characters?

4. What other information do you wish you had about this situation?

5. What seem to be the technical challenges involved in this case?

6. What are the adaptive challenges, and what type of adaptive challenges are they?

7. What risks and opportunities do you see in this case?

8. What biblical and theological principles should be considered in this case?

9. What are your suggested next steps for the parties involved?

10. What longer-term considerations might impact short-term decisions?

11. What work should be given "back to the people" here? To whom, and how?

12. What assumptions and values guide your recommended course of action?

13. What responses did you notice within yourself as you read this case?

14. Do you think anything could have been done differently, either individually or organizationally, to avoid this situation? If so, what?

15. Might this case be different if:

    a) Terry Slayton had been part of the Findlay campus process in some role from the very beginning?

    b) Any one of the entities involved (LTS, ECoC, Home Missions Council, Findlay Campus, Inc.) had full authority over the project?

    c) The Findlay site still showed financial promise?

16. Issues to consider:

    a) Where and how does faith express itself in an organization as it pertains to finances? Where is the line between stepping out in faith and taking a dangerous risk?

    b) How should an organization deal with oppositional views within leadership about a major decision?

    c) What is the conversation stopper in your organization or tribe—the phrase or concept that immediately shuts down charitable discussion?

Commentary

This case pertains to a graduate theological and ministry training school. However, the issues presented here could apply to any church or parachurch ministry seeking to expand its operations and physical presence to other locations. These situations are complex and complicated because of the necessary involvement and oversight of multiple entities; in this case, state and national governing bodies, the LTS president and board, the Findlay Campus board, LTS staff, the denomination, its pastors, the Home Missions Council, and a bank.

In this situation, there are good and godly people landing on different sides of an issue. Is the Findlay campus a missional move or a distraction from the mission? What constitutes good stewardship, and what if the answer is different depending on perspective? In a multiplayer partnership, what if what is best for one entity becomes detrimental to another? The Findlay campus situation has become its own complex system in which every change changes everything.

In addition, the theological differences in understanding the role of faith have widened the divide by moralizing the conflict. Every organization or tribe has a conversation stopper—a term, phrase, or accusation that can immediately end discussion. For some in the Findlay situation, it was "God told us to do this." How can someone argue against that? Other conversation stoppers might include phrases such as "it's not biblical" or labeling or accusing people and positions using what are known as loaded terms. These words or phrases elicit strong emotional responses, have different interpretations depending on the group defining the term, and serve as boundaries determining who is in or out, right or wrong. Current examples of this might include *liberal*, *gospel*, *evangelical*, and *woke*.

All this is to say that whereas the original idea regarding the Findlay site seemed to be a win-win, it now appears that at least one party may lose, whether in terms of financial income and stability, leadership trust and goodwill, and/or institutional impact and reach. In addition, a win in one area may result in a loss in another. For example, LTS could regain financial stability and independence, but at high relational cost with board members, area pastors, and donors.

One thing is certain: large projects such as this take a lot of leadership time and energy, and they almost never go as smoothly, as cheaply, or as quickly as planned.

ADDITIONAL QUESTIONS

1. Has your initial diagnosis of this situation changed? If so, how and why?

2. Which character(s) do you find yourself empathizing with?

3. Do you need to revise or address any of your assumptions?

Epilogue

The Findlay campus was developed on the belief that it would bring more money to LTS. However, as the May board meeting approached, Terry became convinced that LTS's continued involvement with Findlay was now an albatross for the school. While as president he held the authority to make a unilateral decision about LTS's operational relationship to the Findlay site, he decided that he was still new enough in his presidency that he should involve the board in the decision.

In conversations prior to the board gathering, Terry let

members know that he was going to bring a recommendation on behalf of the LTS staff that the school cease operations at the Findlay site. In response, several board members announced that they would not attend the board gathering, and a few others chose to attend only for the first day of discussion and not for the second day when a vote would be taken.

By the end of the first day of discussion, the board was leaning toward continuing the relationship with the Findlay campus for one more year. Board members from the east-central region strongly advocated for the ongoing relationship, insisting that it could become profitable. But in the absence of several of these members the next day, the board members in attendance ultimately decided to cease operations at the Findlay site. Because higher education was becoming more distributed, more organic, and less tied to bricks-and-mortar campuses, the overarching feeling among those in the conversation was that the Findlay campus was now an anchor, not an opportunity.

While Terry was convinced the decision was the right one, it came at a high cost. Over the next few years, between resignations and normal attrition, board membership dropped from seventeen or eighteen members to seven or eight. LTS lost donors who were primarily committed to the Findlay site. As giving declined, LTS authorized emergency use of its endowment to cover operating costs. This drained the fund to only $15,000, with board permission to spend it down to zero if needed. In addition, leaders in the east-central region of the ECoC decided to take back a nondegree pastoral training program that they had given to LTS decades earlier, thereby removing this revenue stream for LTS.

But the biggest challenge for Terry was sorting out and rebuilding relationships that had been damaged through the process. At the time of the Findlay decision, Terry made two commitments: First, whatever decision was made, he and the current leaders at LTS would stand by it, answer questions, receive whatever criticism came their way, and learn from it. Second, Terry would not fight. At times, the second commitment worked against him because he was sometimes misrepresented as not caring when he was trying to respect the polity and authority of other individuals and organizations.

It took years of conversations and explanations with board members, pastors, and donors to turn the situation around. LTS has regained fiscal soundness, with increased enrollment, new and returning donors, and $2.2 million in its endowment. Only a few LTS staff remain from the days of the Findlay decision. The board has brought on new members, although there is a clear delineation between those who know what the organization went through and those who do not. Finally, the majority of relationships with former board members and other parties have also been restored.

Terry Slayton is in his seventh year as president at Lambert Theological School. For a time, Findlay was "that which shall not be named" within LTS. However, Terry worked to ensure that conversations remained open and honest, knowing that at some point he might be the person to bring a $5 million dream to the board and that the organization would need to know how to have deep discussions about big ideas.

Meanwhile, the Findlay campus continues to operate, although it is no longer affiliated with LTS in any way. Under the leadership of president Cam Newberg, the site now operates as a Christian academy for grades nine through twelve and as an extension site for another seminary that is not affiliated with LTS or the ECoC. It continues to pay interest to the Home Missions Council for the loan to purchase the property.

As later conversations revealed, Newberg was heavily

influenced by the work of Clayton Christensen and his concept of disruptive innovation. Newberg had conceived of the Findlay campus as a way to bring change to LTS via the creation of a separate and innovative entity, rather than trying to change the larger, existing LTS organization. However, Newberg had not explained this theoretical framework to others when he began implementing his plan for change through the Findlay site. LTS thought it was opening an extension site at Findlay for additional revenue, while the institution's appointed leader for the effort had a different agenda.

All parties involved still believe they were right.

Now What?

1. How do you feel now that you've read the entire case and know how it ended?

2. Would you have acted similarly?

3. How could a different result have been achieved?

4. What actions can you, your fellow leaders, and your organization take to prepare for—and perhaps avoid, mitigate, or replicate—this particular situation or outcome?

Recommended Resources

Christensen, Clayton M. *The Innovator's Dilemma: When New Technologies Cause Great Firms to Fail*. Management of Innovation and Change. Boston: Harvard Business Review Press, 2015.

Duck, Jeanie Daniel. *The Change Monster: The Human Forces That Fuel or Foil Corporate Transformation and Change.* New York: Three Rivers Press, 2001.

Parker, Marsha. *Shared Governance for Beginners: Six Competencies for a Quick Start.* Shared Governance Practitioner. North Charleston, SC: CreateSpace, 2016.

16 ALL FOR ONE?

Caitlyn Lowe was twenty-four years old and in her first staff position at a church, serving as youth pastor. As she prepared for her first summer on the job, Caitlyn decided to take a team of ten students from the youth group on a weeklong missions trip to a third-world country. While there, the students would do hut-to-hut evangelism, lead vacation Bible school (VBS), and deliver meals to families in need. It would be the perfect combination of service and leadership. Caitlyn had participated on numerous such trips through her teen years and as a student at college and seminary. While leading an entire trip was a new experience, she felt reasonably confident in her knowledge and skill.

Until she began to receive registrations for the trip.

Emily had been involved in the youth program for the past four years. During that time, she had had multiple altercations with other youth, including verbal yelling matches and physical fights. To Caitlyn, it seemed that Emily started some sort of big drama among different students every few weeks. Emily seemed to have had some growth in her relationship with Jesus, but the outbursts certainly did not reflect this. Caitlyn knew that Emily had struggled with bipolar disorder, depression, and panic and anxiety attacks since she was a child.

Emily's behavior on the last youth winter retreat included the usual outbursts and drama. During free time, when no adults were around, she started a shouting match with several other girls that involved cussing, accusing, and dishonesty. Another student happened to record the interaction. Once Caitlyn and another adult reviewed it, they sat the girls down to hear their sides of the story. Emily denied that anything had happened or that she had done anything bad. She was rude and disrespectful toward the other girls as well as toward the adult leaders. Once Emily found out the adults had seen a recording of the incident, she tried to twist the story to blame everything on the other girls and came up with a reason why she had to yell and use that kind of language. During that conversation, all girls were told that this was their final warning before calling parents to have them picked up. Later that evening during a big group worship session, Emily broke down crying and asked for forgiveness from the other girls as well as from Jesus.

On the way home from the retreat, Emily once again instigated drama with a few girls in the back of the church van. Because of the shouting, the gossip, and the lies, Emily had created a sour ending to a weekend that had been incredibly important to many other students' faith.

The forthcoming missions trip had been advertised as open to anyone in grades nine to twelve. During the informational meeting a few weeks earlier, many of the students were very excited as they discussed whether they were going and signed up. Emily was also excited as she talked to Caitlyn about wanting to join the team. After the informational meeting, Emily's mom, Barb, had informed Caitlyn that Emily has never been out of the country but was looking forward to going on the trip. A church family had already informed Barb that they would pay for half of Emily's trip. Barb was living paycheck to paycheck as a single mom and did not have the money for costs that were not covered by the planned fundraisers.

Given Emily's long-term and recent behavior, as well as her family situation, should Caitlyn allow her to join the missions team? One the one hand, an experience like this trip could be life-changing for Emily. Serving those less fortunate, being immersed in poverty, and being part of a team that cared for her could show her God's love and give her purpose.

God promised that people who have a relationship with Jesus become a new creation (2 Cor. 5:17). Caitlyn knew that God had done and would continue to do miracles in people. Should Caitlyn therefore allow Emily to join the team and trust that God will provide the money and change Emily's heart, attitude, and actions by the time the team left for the trip?

Jesus asked his followers to forgive "seventy times seven times," but he also said that repentance would result in changed behavior. Emily had been forgiven and given countless chances. But if she continued to demonstrate the same behaviors over and over, had she truly repented and turned around?

Just as important, though, Caitlyn desired unity for the team. She wanted the teens to be likeminded, loving, compassionate, and humble (1 Peter 3:8), forgiving, and "united in mind and thought" (1 Cor. 1:10). Was Emily's potential drama enough to affect team unity and ruin the trip for others, similar to what had happened at the winter retreat?

From a financial standpoint, asking for monetary support for a missions trip could be a great way to learn to depend on Jesus to provide financially and to rely on him for confirmation of whether someone was called to go. Since another church member had already offered to pay for half of Emily's trip, would it be right to ask her not to go, or was that a sign that God was calling her to the team?

Caitlyn realized she had been so concerned about reaching the threshold of ten students for the team that she hadn't thought about designing an application that would explain clear expectations or screen for maturity among team members. She also hadn't thought about someone like Emily signing up. Questions swirled in her head. No matter what was decided, the situation seemed to involve a lot of relational risks along with potential spiritual consequences.

QUESTIONS FOR REFLECTION

1. With the information you've been given, how would you summarize the problem(s) in this case?

2. Who are the main characters and what are their roles in this situation?

3. What assumptions and values do you hear voiced by these characters?

4. What other information do you wish you had about this situation?

5. What seem to be the technical challenges involved in this case?

6. What are the adaptive challenges, and what type of adaptive challenges are they?

7. What risks and opportunities do you see in this case?

8. What biblical and theological principles should be considered in this case?

9. What are your suggested next steps for the parties involved?

10. What longer-term considerations might impact short-term decisions?

11. What work should be given "back to the people" here? To whom, and how?

12. What assumptions and values guide your recommended course of action?

13. What responses did you notice within yourself as you read this case?

14. Do you think anything could have been done differently, either individually or organizationally, to avoid this situation? If so, what?

15. Might this case be different if:

    a) Caitlyn were older?

    b) Caitlyn were a man?

    c) Emily's mother, Barb, were a Christian?

    d) The trip were only service oriented with no leadership responsibilities given to the students?

    e) The trip were to take place within the United States and not to a foreign country?

16. Issues to consider:

a) How does a leader choose between the needs of the individual and the needs of a group?

b) What are the best practices for training and mentoring a young or an inexperienced ministry leader?

c) What (if any) standards of spiritual and emotional maturity should be used when selecting people for volunteer ministry or service? How might these be evaluated?

Commentary

As a new leader, Caitlyn is learning on the job, and she has already learned a lot from this situation. In hindsight, she realizes she should have developed an application process that considers a potential team member's maturity and should have communicated standards and expectations around individual behaviors and team unity. To this point, she has sat alone with her concerns, unaware whether the church has any policy or philosophy to guide this type of decision. She alone feels the acute tension of wanting the best for the team yet also wanting to provide opportunity and hope for Emily and her mother.

It seems her instincts as a leader and her heart as a pastor are in conflict. Either choice feels like a risk. And as a young pastor in her first staff role, she feels that this decision carries even more weight. Caitlyn will need to engage others from the church in the decision, and hopefully they can decide together what is a loving and redemptive response. It should be noted that although this case concerns a youth ministry situation, the issues in this case are common to all areas of ministry.

---

1. Has your initial diagnosis of this situation changed? If so, how and why?

2. Which character(s) do you find yourself empathizing with?

3. Do you need to revise or address any of your assumptions?

Epilogue

It turned out that Caitlyn did not have to deliberate for long. The following week at work, the executive pastor declared that Emily would not be able to go on the trip. He was aware of the previous issues with Emily and felt the potential liability of her participation was just too great. He told Caitlyn she would need to inform Emily and Barb. Caitlyn's internal tension only increased. While she felt it was probably best that Emily was not allowed on the trip and was glad the decision was made for her, she still felt terrible about having to disappoint Emily and her mother and was concerned about how Barb would respond. Nevertheless, she contacted Barb and scheduled a meeting at a coffee shop.

When they sat down together, Barb knew immediately what was going on. "You're not letting her go on the trip, are you," she said, and it was not really a question. Caitlyn acknowledged the decision but wanted to discuss the concerns with Barb. The single mother would have none of it. "This happens at every church," she said angrily. The conversation was over almost as quickly as it had begun. Barb left the coffee shop, and Emily and Barb never attended that church again.

| Now What? |

1. How do you feel now that you've read the entire case and know how it ended?

2. Would you have acted similarly?

3. How could a different result have been achieved?

4. What actions can you, your fellow leaders, and your organization take to prepare for—and perhaps avoid, mitigate, or replicate—this particular situation or outcome?

Recommended Resources

Ellis, Lynne, and Doug Fields. *Mission Trips from Start to Finish: How to Organize and Lead Impactful Mission Trips.* Loveland, CO: Group Publishing, 2008.

Ortlund, Dane. *Gentle and Lowly: The Heart of Christ for Sinners and Sufferers.* Wheaton, IL: Crossway, 2020.

Shelley, Marshall. *Ministering to Problem People in Your Church: What to Do with Well-Intentioned Dragons.* Minneapolis: Bethany, 2013.

17 | FUTURE TENSE

While some adaptive challenges present as one-time or acute problems in need of quick decisions, many real-life situations unfold over a longer period of time. In these cases, new information can add layers of nuance and complexity to the situation, sometimes even changing the real challenge. Meanwhile, the people involved in the situation also continue to evolve, leading to shifting emotional and relational dynamics, and sometimes even the departure of key characters while the story is still being written. Decisions lead to new consequences and sometimes to new adaptive challenges.

The following case unfolds in this fashion, with several intermediate reflection points added for you to make initial determinations, then to revisit those as the story unfolds.

Founded seventy-five years ago, To All Mission (TAM) grew out of the vision of committed believers in a church Sunday school class and their desire to reach the world for Christ. At that time, one of the group members asked his close friends to support him and send him to Brazil. He already knew Spanish and believed that learning Portuguese was not too far of a stretch. The group organized to funnel financial support to this man, and thus TAM was born.

In TAM's earliest days, volunteers spent several hours per week processing donations, writing thank-you letters to donors, and promoting the ministry. Over time, the "we will support you" founding mentality solidified, and TAM focused on sending people wherever they desired to minister. TAM neither interfered with nor restricted their ministry.

Fifty years after its founding, the number of missionaries supported through TAM had grown to more than 125. The men and women who started the ministry retired, and the leadership mantle was passed to new members from the founding church who held the missiological priorities. One of these transitions included the longtime chairman of the board, who had served for thirty-five years. The board selected a new chairman, Frank McDowell, who also had a high commitment to maintaining peace and past practices.

However, times had changed. After September 2011, new regulations for international financial transactions meant more work for the organization to handle the finances, taxes, and administration associated with its ministry. TAM started charging a 15 percent administrative fee and had to hire part-time staff to do the work formerly completed by volunteers, both of which took a bite out of gross donations. Although TAM did an adequate job of managing donors, accounting, and finance, the organization provided few other services. It continued to function primarily as a financial processing agency.

Throughout its history, TAM's leadership emphasized a commitment to what had worked in the past. In keeping with its origins, the organization was volunteer driven, loosely structured, and relational, with few policies, procedures, or guidelines. The leaders tended to resist suggestions that would make the ministry feel "too organizational." As a result, the organization languished and then stagnated as it clung to the past.

| Initial Questions for Reflection |

1. With the information you've been given, how would you summarize the problem(s) in this case?

2. What other information do you wish you had about this situation?

3. What seem to be the technical challenges involved in this case?

4. What are the adaptive challenges, and what type of adaptive challenges are they?

5. What would be your recommended course of action at this point?

In 2015, the board recognized the need for an executive director to guide TAM into the future. With a desire to increase the number of missionaries and with deep experience in missions, the new executive director, Ian Whitlock, focused on mobilization of new missionaries to new frontiers. Blessed with a big vision, Ian worked with the board to extend TAM's reach beyond the scope of its work to that point—which had been driven by each missionary's agenda—and to the unreached. Ian wanted to engage the world in discipleship, evangelism, and church planting. He wanted to open the organizational doors to anyone who felt called to missions but was unable to go because of restrictions or limitations from other missions agencies. With this big vision, he challenged the board to grow and enlisted five new staff members to serve with TAM.

Frank, the board chairman, verbally embraced these changes. He said they were long overdue, although he also wanted to maintain continuity with and a commitment to past practices. Frank avoided conflict and wanted everyone to just have a sweet spirit. Meanwhile, other board members and staff wondered how the missionaries would respond to a new emphasis on unreached people groups (UPGs). Most of TAM's missionaries worked in their own self-defined traditional missionary roles, aligned with projects such as building and maintaining schools, orphanages, and other ministries. Outside of a few exceptions, none of TAM's missionaries had focused on UPGs.

Concerned that the men and women they classified as "our" missionaries might not understand the shift in focus, TAM's leadership was hesitant to give clear direction or instruction to the field. The pattern had been set since its founding: TAM functioned as a missions financial management company facilitating the work of others, not as a missions sending agency.

With Ian's desire to focus on the unreached but not upset the missionaries, he proposed a new enlistment plan for new personnel to work with the unreached. With this plan, TAM could let their current missionaries continue their work while also mobilizing new personnel toward the unreached. Frank, not wanting conflict, also agreed with the idea.

Ian needed research to identify new people groups in cutting-edge locations for these prospective new personnel. He asked a friend, Patrick McCall, to provide him with a list of all UPGs with more than one hundred thousand people. Patrick responded with a list of three thousand unreached groups, which were too many for an agency to focus on. When Patrick asked about criteria to narrow the list for an unreached emphasis, Ian could not verbalize a clear direction or filter the three thousand unreached peoples to chart a focus for TAM.

Each time it was discussed, Ian spoke about a need for mobilization. The staff attempted to bring focus and decide on an emphasis, but none met Ian's approval, although he could not articulate why he disagreed with these proposals. Ian continued to talk about TAM's vision to reach the world but lapsed back to his experience as a missionary thirty-five years earlier. The staff and board became increasingly frustrated by their executive director's lack of direction and decisiveness. Staff members became more dismissive of Ian because he rambled through meetings recounting his experiences on the field.

CONTINUED INITIAL QUESTIONS

1. With this additional information, how would you summarize the problem(s) in this case?

2. Would you change your initial assessment of the nature of challenges in this case? (Which are technical, which are adaptive, and what type of adaptive challenges are they?)

3. Who are the main characters and what are their roles in this situation?

4. What assumptions and values do you hear voiced by these characters?

5. What other information do you wish you had about this situation?

6. What would be your recommended course of action at this point?

Concerns became more obvious as TAM relocated to another state. The wife of TAM's founder had passed away, and the founder wanted to move back to his home state. The board approved TAM's relocation; however, to do so the organization would need to incorporate as a new organization in the new state. This meant that the old organizing documents and policies, which had been grandfathered in over the years by the state in which TAM had been founded, would need to be rewritten for the new state, with significantly increased legal requirements.

These requirements would also necessitate a restructuring of the board, which had to this time consisted of eight members. Four of these were employees at TAM, while the other four had been recruited by Ian. To comply with the legal requirements in the new state of incorporation, the board would need to consist of "disinterested parties" who were neither employees of TAM nor cronies of the executive director. The board would also need to institute term limits: as originally constituted, board members could serve indefinitely, which meant that Frank was in his fifteenth year on the board, with others serving even longer.

In addition, TAM's membership in the Evangelical Council for Financial Accountability (ECFA) required the organization to submit to annual audits, including a review of its organizational governance structure and practices.

As these prospective changes loomed, Ian announced his forthcoming retirement, declared his chosen successor, and stated his desire to remain with TAM as a volunteer mobilizer. Meanwhile, the organization continued to struggle: 60 percent of its missionaries were not meeting their funding goals, which meant that TAM was not receiving the full 15 percent administrative fee it took from gross donations to cover operating expenses. However, TAM continued to take on new missionaries, thereby increasing administrative expenses without commensurate additional income because the new missionaries needed time to build up their financial support. The board treasurer sounded the alarm about the organization's financial situation, but Ian and Frank dismissed the concerns.

QUESTIONS FOR REFLECTION

1. With all available information now presented, how would you summarize the problem(s) in this case?

2. Who are the main characters and what are their roles in this situation?

3. What assumptions and values do you hear voiced by these characters?

4. Review again your assessment of the type and nature of the challenges in this case.

5. What risks and opportunities do you see in this case?

6. What biblical and theological principles should be considered in this case?

7. What are your suggested next steps for the parties involved?

8. What longer-term considerations might impact short-term decisions?

9. What work should be given "back to the people" here? To whom, and how?

10. What assumptions and values guide your recommended course of action?

11. What responses did you notice within yourself as you read this case?

12. Do you think anything could have been done differently, either individually or organizationally, to avoid this situation? If so, what?

13. Might this case be different if:

    a) Ian planned to stay in his role as executive director instead of retiring?

    b) TAM were able to meet its budget?

    c) TAM planned to stay in its home state?

14. Issues to consider:

    a) Who is responsible for setting and communicating organizational direction? Should it be the executive director, the board, or the staff, or some combination? What are the advantages and disadvantages to any of these options?

    b) When is a posture of keeping the peace healthy, and when is it detrimental? What do healthy disagreement and conflict look like?

    c) What are the criteria to determine whether an organization needs to stay the same, make changes, or disband?

Commentary

TAM is like many aging organizations in that it needs to modernize its strategy and operations, while its leaders are resistant to change. TAM was founded with an inspiring motive: to help send missionaries around the world, to whatever location and type of ministry the missionaries felt called. But all organizations must adapt and change as they grow and as their context changes. As missiological perspectives and priorities shift globally, TAM must evaluate and clarify its mission, values, and strategies. And as legal requirements change, TAM must adjust its organizational structure and operating model to comply while not compromising its mission or financial viability.

There is no doubt that TAM needs to make significant changes going forward. The biggest question is who will lead those efforts. To this point, the executive director and board members have resisted modernization for a variety of reasons, including fear of becoming too organizational, fear of conflict, fear of making a decision, and fear of deviating from TAM's purpose and strategy. It seems that the leaders are frozen by their relationships. And with no term limits, there is no fresh blood to bring new perspectives and weight; the leadership just recycles itself.

Ian has announced his resignation, which may bring hope that a new executive director might be able to lead change. However, the same board that is resistant to change will also be responsible for hiring a new executive director, so there is no guarantee that they will hire a director who would want to deviate significantly from the status quo. And yet to even continue to exist, the organization *must* change to meet operating requirements in its new location. It remains to be seen whether TAM's leadership will run the organization into the ground by clinging to the past or will finally recognize the urgency of the situation and agree to make significant changes.

| ADDITIONAL QUESTIONS |

1. Has your initial diagnosis of this situation changed? If so, how and why?

2. Which character(s) do you find yourself empathizing with?

3. Do you need to revise or address any of your assumptions?

Epilogue

TAM enlisted several consultants to rewrite the bylaws to comply with the regulations of the organization's new home state and the ECFA. Their revision included several key changes:

1. Term limits for members to consist of three-year terms, renewable two times for up to nine years of consecutive service.
2. Clarification of roles: The board would oversee organizational governance, while staff would oversee the day-to-day operations of the organization. Ian's handpicked successor, Steve Schaefer, would hold the position of chief executive officer (CEO) of the organization.
3. A smaller board consisting of a majority of disinterested parties who were not on staff and could not benefit financially or otherwise from their role on the board. Steve, as CEO, and TAM's treasurer would be the only staff members who also held seats on the board.
4. Elimination of private benefit (legally known as inurement) for staff members, who had previously been allowed to donate to the organization and receive those funds to their missionary accounts.

The consultants sent their proposal to the board for consideration at its next regularly scheduled gathering. They knew the proposed changes were necessary for compliance with governing and overseeing entities but were not sure whether board members would be willing to accept these changes.

Over two days of meetings, the conversations among board members grew increasingly contentious. Frank wanted the board to continue to direct everyday operations of the organization under his oversight, as had been the practice during his previous fifteen years as chairman. Other board members felt the organization needed to accept the proposed changes to ensure TAM's sustainable future, although a key point in the conversation was how close the organization could skirt requirements while staying legally compliant.

As push came to shove, the previously conflict-avoidant Frank changed tactics and escalated the conflict by attempting to manipulate other board members toward his point of view and by disparaging the consultants. When these efforts were unsuccessful, he offered to resign but then rescinded, declaring that the others would have to force him off the board.

At that point Steve, the newly appointed CEO, spoke up. "We're not going to do this," he announced. "We are going to walk out of here united, together. Frank, you can no longer serve on this board." At that, Frank resigned and left the meeting.

Meanwhile, Ian maintained that he wanted to stay with the organization in a "mobilization" role now that he had stepped down as president. Yet in conversations about what that role might entail, no one could determine measurable outcomes. It seemed that Ian just wanted to meet with people and encourage them, without any clear value to the organization. With this being his last board meeting and with no official role for him in the future, Ian quickly disengaged from the discussions. A third board member also resigned, stating he was tired of the drama he experienced during his four years of service.

The remaining board members approved the new bylaws with minimal revisions. Now, without its longtime former board chair and previous president, Steve has begun the work of building a healthy, modern organization that is structured appropriately to serve its missionaries.

┤ NOW WHAT? ├

1. How do you feel now that you've read the entire case and know how it ended?

2. Would you have acted similarly?

3. How could a different result have been achieved?

4. What actions can you, your fellow leaders, and your organization take to prepare for—and perhaps avoid, mitigate, or replicate—this particular situation or outcome?

Recommended Resources

Bridges, William. *Managing Transitions: Making the Most of Change.* 25th anniv. ed. Boston: Da Capo Press, 2017.

Evangelical Council for Financial Accountability. "ECFA's Integrity Standards for Nonprofits," www.ecfa.org/Standards.aspx.

Kotter, John P. *Leading Change.* Boston: Harvard Business Review Press, 2012.

WHO STOLE MY CHURCH?

Oak Creek Community Church was founded in the early 1980s by pastor Jerry Vanderberg in a rapidly growing suburb of a rapidly growing city. In addition to starting Oak Creek Church, Jerry was instrumental in the founding of a new regional denomination, the Evangelical Reformed Church (ERC), and in leading Oak Creek Church to start a Christian school, Oak Creek Christian School, which met in the church's facilities. During thirty-one years of faithful ministry, Oak Creek Church built a legacy of excellence and influence in its suburb and beyond, while Jerry became a beloved and highly influential figure in the church, the community, and the denomination. When he retired, thousands honored him locally and around the world. It was clear the church had massive shoes to fill.

After a lengthy national search with the help of a first-rate search firm, Oak Creek found Jerry's successor: Brady Dugan, a forty-two-year-old rising star who was plucked from the staff of a nationally known nondenominational megachurch. Brady was unanimously approved by the Oak Creek board of elders, and the congregation rejoiced over its good fortune and bright future.

Under Brady's leadership on the foundation of Jerry's legacy, Oak Creek Church experienced a new season of rapid growth. One year after Brady's arrival, Oak Creek Church was recognized as the fastest growing church in the country. On the outside, it seemed that God was abundantly blessing the church and Brady's leadership.

On the inside, however, rumblings had begun. In Brady's first few months on the job, he had made some unpopular staffing moves, including releasing some longtime staff members in favor of bringing in his own people from his former church. Compared with Jerry Vanderberg's measured demeanor, Brady was a strong personality with unflinching boldness in pursuit of what he felt God was calling the church to become.

A few years into his tenure, Brady was convicted that most of Oak Creek Church's rapid growth was because of transfer growth from other churches in the area and Christians who were new to town. After attending a conference at a well-known, controversial charismatic church, during which he experienced spontaneous healing of a physical ailment, he became convinced that Oak Creek Church needed a fresh movement of the Holy Spirit. He called the congregation to forty days of prayer, and that's when strange things started to happen.

It began with a week of evening prayer meetings. Hundreds of attendees reported genuine physical healing and spiritual revival. Obeying what he felt was God's direction and clear blessing, Brady decided to continue the nightly revivals for months. The church started a 24/7 prayer movement. People were coming to faith or renewing their commitment to Christ in droves. In just one year, the church recorded nearly six thousand salvation decisions, several thousand of those over one weekend of multiple Christmas services. Word was getting out around town about the revivals and about how Oak Creek Church was becoming charismatic.

As unfamiliar as this was to Brady from his mainstream megachurch experience, it was completely foreign to the pre-existing culture and leadership of Oak Creek Church. The theological stream with which the church was affiliated, and the denomination Jerry had helped found, had no context for the wild movement of the Holy Spirit, for speaking in tongues, for miraculous healing. Their stream was known for doing all things decently and in order. Oak Creek Church was becoming something completely different from what it had been and what it was supposed to be.

Rumors started flying: Brady was disregarding and disrespecting the leadership of the elders under the church's governance structure. He wanted to remove the church from the ERC and go nondenominational. He wanted to make the church seeker-driven, like his previous church. He was an authoritarian leader and guilty of emotional and spiritual abuse toward staff. He claimed to be a prophet. He wanted the Oak Creek School to vacate its building so he could turn it into a school for supernatural ministry.

But there were also voices on the other side: Brady was the leader Oak Creek Church needed to bring revival to the congregation. He was being used by God to bring thousands to Christ. He was just a humble servant doing what he felt God was leading him to do. God was pruning the church of dead weight.

It was true that many new people were coming to Christ and to the church. It was also true that many longtime members were leaving and that the elders were growing increasingly displeased with Brady's leadership.

QUESTIONS FOR REFLECTION

1. With the information you've been given, how would you summarize the problem(s) in this case?

2. Who are the main characters and what are their roles in this situation?

3. What assumptions and values do you hear voiced by these characters?

4. What other information do you wish you had about this situation?

5. What seem to be the technical challenges involved in this case?

6. What are the adaptive challenges, and what type of adaptive challenges are they?

7. What risks and opportunities do you see in this case?

8. What biblical and theological principles should be considered in this case?

9. What are your suggested next steps for the parties involved?

10. What longer-term considerations might impact short-term decisions?

11. What work should be given "back to the people" here? To whom, and how?

12. What assumptions and values guide your recommended course of action?

13. What responses did you notice within yourself as you read this case?

14. Do you think anything could have been done differently, either individually or organizationally, to avoid this situation? If so, what?

15. Might this case be different if:

   a) Oak Creek Church were nondenominational or a member of a charismatic denomination?

   b) The church were not experiencing revival under Brady's leadership?

   c) Brady had not been the unanimous choice by the elders to replace Jerry Vanderberg?

   d) Brady's personality were more similar to Jerry's?

16. Issues to consider:

   a) What can be done if an organization's senior leader seems to "go rogue"? Who determines the boundaries?

   b) What is the best way to distinguish fact from fiction in a conflict when each person has their own perspective?

   c) What principles should guide who should set vision and direction for an organization? Should it be a senior pastor/director, or the board? What are the advantages and disadvantages to each? Are there other models that should be considered?

Commentary

Is Brady sinful or just out of sync with the older members' desires and the denomination's systems, structures, and traditions? Is he arrogantly going off on his own or simply obeying God's direction instead of bowing to human criticism? What obligation does Brady have to follow established governing structures and authorities while following the Holy Spirit? Does the Holy Spirit work within established structures, or are they a hindrance to his movement?

At the very least, it seems that Brady is a gross mismatch for what Oak Creek Community Church thinks it wants and believed it was getting when they hired him. Whether or not his behavior would be considered sinful or faithful in God's eyes, the reality is that Brady is ministering in the context of a human-led local church that is part of a very orderly, noncharismatic denomination, and right now those systems feel that Brady is out of order. If the revival was a work of God, it seems that reconciliation between the two sides will require an even greater miracle.

ADDITIONAL QUESTIONS

1. Has your initial diagnosis of this situation changed? If so, how and why?

2. Which character(s) do you find yourself empathizing with?

3. Do you need to revise or address any of your assumptions?

Epilogue

Seven years after Brady arrived, the battle lines had been clearly drawn. On one side stood the elders and longtime congregants who felt Brady was taking their church in the wrong direction. On the other stood those who had come to the church and to Christ as a result of Brady's ministry and who wondered why this impact was being questioned.

Both sides took their arguments to the internet. One

social-media group claimed that Brady was being persecuted. Another circulated a petition asking people to sign a plea for Brady to resign immediately because his failed leadership had put the church in crisis. Jerry Vanderberg's wife even got involved, writing an open letter to Brady asking him to stop ruining the church her husband had founded and pastored.

In midsummer of that year, as the church was still holding revival services six evenings per week, the elders brought multiple formal charges against Brady via the denominational process. These charges included false teaching, intimidation and fear-based leadership, and lack of submission, among others. He was asked to repent or resign. Brady did neither, claiming that he had been charged unfairly, that the accusations were false, and that he had not been given the opportunity to respond to each of the charges. He maintained that under those circumstances, he could not in good conscience choose either of the options presented to him.

At this, the board of elders resigned en masse and appealed to the denomination for intervention, saying Brady was above accountability and they could not work with him. Denominational authorities installed an emergency group of elders who were chosen from among pastors and lay leaders in the local judicatory. After spending a month reviewing the evidence they had received, the ad hoc elders suspended Brady as lead pastor of Oak Creek Community Church.

By this time, however, Brady had a big enough following among congregants and staff that the risk of a church split was very real, and no one desired that. The denomination provided temporary pastoral leadership and preaching while it continued to work with the church and with Brady on a viable solution. The leaders soon decided that Oak Creek Community Church would release and bless Brady to start a new church in the area, one that fit Brady's sense of call and style of ministry.

One month after his suspension, Brady launched the new Riverview Church with more than five hundred attendees, multiple staff, and full funding. That church continues to grow steadily.

Meanwhile, Oak Creek Community Church commenced a search for its next lead pastor, who was installed one year after Brady's departure. Oak Creek Church has also resumed its growth, with many former members returning to their longtime church home.

Now What?

1. How do you feel now that you've read the entire case and know how it ended?

2. Would you have acted similarly?

3. How could a different result have been achieved?

4. What actions can you, your fellow leaders, and your organization take to prepare for—and perhaps avoid, mitigate, or replicate—this particular situation or outcome?

Recommended Resources

Cymbala, Jim. *Fresh Wind, Fresh Fire: What Happens When God's Spirit Invades the Hearts of His People.* Updated and expanded. Grand Rapids: Zondervan, 2018.

Vanderbloemen, William, and Warren Bird. *Next: Pastoral Succession That Works.* Grand Rapids: Baker, 2014.

Van Yperen, Jim. *Making Peace: A Guide to Overcoming Church Conflict.* Chicago: Moody, 2002.

UNDER DECONSTRUCTION

The Table was a small, organic faith community started by a gifted young couple, Ryan and Tara Rose, who left an established church in the Bible Belt to start a small missional community in a large progressive city. The Table was one of a number of experimental communities being established around the country as young Christian leaders were asking fresh questions about the gospel and culture.

The Table grew steadily from its first days in the Roses' living room, soon renting space for a weekly worship gathering while continuing house gatherings during the week. After a few years of the church's slow growth, Ryan invited a longtime friend and former colleague, Chris Walden, to move to the city to serve as the church's lead pastor.

The Table had been established as a 501(c)3 not-for-profit organization, with Ryan as its president. As such, he was the legal chair of its board and the de facto head of The Table. Because of Ryan and Tara's connections from previous ministry and their innovative ministry with The Table, Ryan and Tara began receiving speaking invitations from around the country. Hiring Chris would free up the couple to travel while Chris tended to the everyday leadership of the church. Ryan would serve as a sort of copastor and worship leader as his availability permitted. And the two men would be reunited in ministry, which had been an ongoing dream of theirs since their first experience serving together at a church.

Chris and his wife excitedly made the 1,200-mile move to join the Roses at The Table. Within six months, however, Chris noticed subtle signs that not only were he and Ryan not on the same page as to how to lead a church but they were starting to move in different directions theologically. Still, since Ryan was frequently on the road, those differences didn't really affect the day-to-day leadership of The Table.

Over the next few years, the church continued to grow and to take a more established form, which included the hiring of several additional staff and the formation of a leadership team for accountability. The congregation was flourishing, and The Table's national profile was growing. Chris fielded emails from leaders around the country who had heard about this unique church and wanted to know more.

Meanwhile, though, Ryan's spiritual journey seemed to be taking him away from The Table's orthodox theological foundations. Chris grew more concerned about what Ryan might say anytime he preached or led worship.

Things came to a head while Chris was out of town and Ryan took leadership of that week's worship gathering. Toward the conclusion of his sermon, Ryan told the congregation he wanted to talk to the congregation as just a regular person and not as the leader of the church. He then explained how he recently had a spiritual experience and that, as a result, he wasn't sure he still believed in God.

A few hours later while on vacation with his family, Chris received a text from Ryan: "I think things just got really messed up."

QUESTIONS FOR REFLECTION

1. With the information you've been given, how would you summarize the problem(s) in this case?

2. Who are the main characters and what are their roles in this situation?

3. What assumptions and values do you hear voiced by these characters?

4. What other information do you wish you had about this situation?

5. What seem to be the technical challenges involved in this case?

6. What are the adaptive challenges, and what type of adaptive challenges are they?

7. What risks and opportunities do you see in this case?

8. What biblical and theological principles should be considered in this case?

9. What are your suggested next steps for the parties involved?

10. What longer-term considerations might impact short-term decisions?

11. What work should be given "back to the people" here? To whom, and how?

12. What assumptions and values guide your recommended course of action?

13. What responses did you notice within yourself as you read this case?

14. Do you think anything could have been done differently, either individually or organizationally, to avoid this situation? If so, what?

15. Might this case be different if:

    a) Ryan were on staff but not the founder of the church?

    b) Ryan had first expressed his doubts privately to church leaders, not publicly during a worship gathering?

    c) The Table were larger or older?

16. Issues to consider:

    a) How much space for faith questions and doubt is acceptable for the leader of a church or Christian ministry?

    b) When a faith leader expresses a questioning of that faith, how should this be handled by the individual and by the leader's organization, both privately and publicly? Does the degree of doubt matter for how the situation should be handled?

    c) Who gets to decide the theological boundaries for an organization?

Commentary

Ryan is undergoing what is known as deconstruction, a term that had its origins in philosophical and literary criticism but now commonly is used to refer to the process of tearing down and analyzing one's spiritual beliefs and religious experience. During the course of a person's Christian faith journey, questions and doubts are not unusual. But to doubt the existence of God is to question the very foundation of the Christian faith—the foundation on which The Table had presumably been established.

Since Ryan is the founder of The Table, does he get to determine and perhaps change its direction based on his current spirituality? Or is there some sort of theological standard or belief system that The Table has professed and with which leaders are expected to align? The organizational and governing structures seem to be unclear. Ryan is the founder and the legal head of the organization, yet Chris is the lead pastor, although he was hired by and technically reports to Ryan. In addition, the church now has a leadership team that presumably has some oversight, but the extent of its authority is also unclear.

In his public deconstruction confession, Ryan claimed to speak as a regular guy and not as the founder and leader of the community he was speaking to. But in reality, there is no divorcing of the person from the role. Ryan is never *only* the founder and leader of The Table, but he is never *not* the founder and leader. The members of The Table community now have to choose: Will they be loyal to the founder, or to the organization's original vision?

Then there is the matter of Chris and Ryan's personal relationship. The two men have a long and storied leadership relationship, albeit one that was built largely on shared perspectives. If it turns out they are no longer on the same page in significant areas of faith and ministry, what will happen to that friendship?

Further complicating this is The Table's national profile. Chris, Ryan, and the church all have significant influence and a broad following within the alternative church movement. Whatever happens at The Table, a lot of people will be watching.

| ADDITIONAL QUESTIONS |

1. Has your initial diagnosis of this situation changed? If so, how and why?

2. Which character(s) do you find yourself empathizing with?

3. Do you need to revise or address any of your assumptions?

Epilogue

When Chris got back from vacation, he and Ryan sat down to discuss what had happened. Chris expressed his surprise at Ryan's confession and wished he had known more about where Ryan was on his spiritual journey. Ryan acknowledged that he was aware he had dropped a bombshell and offered to step down from leadership at The Table. Chris, still reeling from the revelation, wanting to support his friend, and not wanting any perception of a power grab on his part, declined the offer and reassured Ryan of the community's love for the Rose family— although Chris did ask for no more public surprises. Ryan and Chris also decided they would meet more regularly to reestablish a common vision for The Table.

But while they started to do so with great hope, over the coming months it became painfully clear that the two men had less and less to talk about. They were losing common ground, and the friendship was slowly dying. Both felt tremendous tension not only over the friendship but about the looming matter of the future of The Table. During this time, Ryan and Tara maintained a full travel schedule while Chris continued to lead The Table from day to day.

During this time, it became clear that two versions of The

Table had emerged and were increasingly competing against each other: one committed to the beliefs and practices of historical Christian orthodoxy, and another less committed to orthodoxy than to being a safe place for doubts and questions. While these were not in principle mutually exclusive goals, Ryan and Chris saw that the question of which goal had pride of place made an immense difference in the life of the community.

The Table's bylaws included the historic Apostles' Creed as its statement of faith. However, no one on the leadership team seemed fully aware of the depth of their founder's doubts or was willing to hold him to the statement of faith once he began questioning it. It seemed that two Tables were emerging. Chris was attempting to build the church around the orthodox pillars of the Christian faith, while Ryan was vocalizing his doubts about these beliefs.

Over the course of their working relationship at the church, Ryan would initiate a conversation with Chris every six to nine months to talk about how The Table was doing and where it was headed. The next time Ryan opened the door for this conversation, Chris took the opportunity to vulnerably express the internal conflict he was feeling. He explained that he felt the two of them were in different places and that they should explore what it would look like for The Table to no longer be in the middle of their relationship.

Ryan responded that he felt disappointed, hurt, and betrayed. From his and Tara's perspective, they were being rejected by their longtime friend and potentially by the community they had founded. With the discussion at an impasse, the two men eventually asked the church's leaders to get involved. The leadership team was concerned about the situation but could not see a way forward that would not result in a significant break in relationship between some combination of the Roses, the Waldens, and The Table.

Ryan continued to question everything he once held certain.

This included not only his Christian faith but also his presumptions about the church, leadership, and even relationships. Chris now represented everything Ryan had grown wary of, and he began to trust Chris less and less. Ryan and Tara continued to consider leaving The Table and moving to another city.

After months of nonmovement amid ongoing tension, Chris finally asked Ryan outright to bless his leadership of The Table and to release the congregation and the organization to him as lead pastor. He explained that he had led the church for five years and felt he was known and trusted, plus he had a vision for what the church could become. The congregation needed clear leadership, and Chris needed clarity on his future.

A few weeks later, Ryan called Chris with two suggested solutions: either Ryan could remain president from a distance under the current arrangement, or they could work together to co-appoint someone else to be the president of the organization who would oversee Chris. However, Ryan did not feel comfortable with Chris becoming the head of the organization.

After taking some time to consider these options, Chris informed Ryan that he didn't think he could stay in either scenario. Ryan immediately alerted the leadership team that they had an emergency on their hands. Chris tendered his resignation, but since there was no clear idea about what needed to happen next or what to communicate to the congregation, the leadership team pleaded with him to continue to lead services and preach while Ryan led everything else until they could figure things out. The congregation had no idea that all of this was going on behind the scenes, but for Ryan, Chris, and the leadership team the situation remained tense and exhausting for several weeks as they all considered how to proceed with minimal damage to the church and to personal relationships.

Finally, Ryan called Chris. "I've been thinking, and The Table is now more your dream than it is mine," he conceded. "I think it's time for me to step away." Within a few more weeks, Ryan had signed the organization over to Chris, and the Roses made plans to leave the area. The Table community threw the family a big going-away party. For Chris, this was an awkward time, as some people knew the whole story but many did not. Still, while Chris was tired, he thought he could now look forward to bringing the staff and leadership team together and to leading them unencumbered by the uncertainty that had loomed for several years.

He was not prepared for what came next.

After several years of trauma, Chris likened the first post-Ryan leadership meeting to sitting with a family after one of their loved ones had died. Some were just sad, but others directed angst and animus specifically at Chris. To many of them, Chris had just staged a successful coup against Ryan. One member of the leadership team told Chris, "I will never trust you again."

Chris did his best to lead The Table through a period of recovery. And after a tenuous season, the church did begin to show signs of new life. But after two years of trying to regain trust and lead amid the ongoing narrative of a power grab, Chris and his wife were wounded and exhausted. When they were approached about joining the staff of a different church in a new city, they welcomed the opportunity.

Chris continues to serve at that church today. The Roses continue to speak and travel from what became their new home base. They have returned to The Table several times since Chris's departure. The Roses and the Waldens occasionally keep in touch via text message.

The Table hired a new pastor from within its previous staff and has survived but has never come close to regaining the momentum or attendance it had during its peak. Its viability remains tenuous.

| NOW WHAT? |
---

1. How do you feel now that you've read the entire case and know how it ended?

2. Would you have acted similarly?

3. How could a different result have been achieved?

4. What actions can you, your fellow leaders, and your organization take to prepare for—and perhaps avoid, mitigate, or replicate—this particular situation or outcome?

Recommended Resources

Campolo, Tony, and Bart Campolo. *Why I Left, Why I Stayed: Conversations on Christianity between an Evangelical Father and His Humanist Son.* New York: HarperOne, 2018.

Hagberg, Janet O., and Robert A. Guelich: *The Critical Journey: Stages in the Life of Faith.* 2nd ed. Salem, WI: Sheffield Publishing Co., 2004.

Mesa, Ivan, ed. *Before You Lose Your Faith: Deconstructing Doubt in the Church.* Deerfield, IL: Gospel Coalition, 2021.

CHAPTER

20

IN SICKNESS AND
IN HEALTH

Jared Graff was the senior pastor at Coastal Community Church, a midsized congregation located in a city that was also home to a large regional university. Jared had started out as the youth pastor at Coastal after seminary, working his way to associate pastor and then to senior pastor. His overall tenure at the church spanned sixteen years, eight of those as senior pastor. Thanks to many years of faithful ministry, Jared was a respected and trusted leader both within the church and in the surrounding community. He, his wife, Melissa, and their two children had settled into a happy, fruitful life.

As Jared and Melissa approached their forty-fifth birthdays, Melissa began having some health problems, including joint pain, digestive issues, and exceptional fatigue. All signs pointed to some type of autoimmune disorder. However, despite first-rate care at the neighboring university-hospital system, doctors were unable to arrive at a clear diagnosis. Melissa's health continued to deteriorate to the point where she could hardly get out of bed some days.

When Melissa first fell ill, Jared picked up the family and household responsibilities that had typically fallen to Melissa, such as taking their kids to and from school and extracurricular events, shopping for groceries, and preparing meals. This added stress to his life, but he and Melissa trusted that this would be necessary only for a short season.

However, as Melissa's condition worsened, Jared realized he needed relief from some of his pastoral responsibilities to carry the increased load at home, which included not only household management but also caring for his very sick wife. He asked Coastal's board of trustees for some flexibility in his work schedule, which the board readily approved. The board also asked the church's deacons to set up a meal train to provide several meals per week for the family, and the congregation eagerly responded to the family's needs, with some people also offering to help with transportation and house cleaning. Trustees regularly visited the couple to pray with them and encourage them.

But as weeks turned into months, there was no improvement in Melissa's health. Jared was feeling more and more stressed by the added responsibilities, despite the flexibility granted by the board. He asked for a two-month leave of absence, which the board again granted with full support. During that time, Jared and Melissa sought additional medical treatment and advice; but again, specialists were unable to provide a clear diagnosis, effective treatment, or even a prognosis as to how long this might last. By this time, Melissa was also exhibiting symptoms of clinical depression because she was anxious about the unknown and grieved the loss of her healthy, active life.

Jared returned to the church after his two-month sabbatical just as tired as and more discouraged than when he had left. While Melissa's discouragement had turned into depression, Jared had grown angry at God, frustrated by the lack of answers or healing. He continued to pastor faithfully, but the physical, spiritual, and emotional toll on him was evident. In addition, the family faced mounting medical bills, with no idea how they would cover the costs.

The months turned into a year. Jared and Melissa had tried every intervention they could think of, including traditional medicine, alternative therapies, significant dietary changes, and spiritual healing. Their lives had fallen apart, and the couple had become a shell of their former selves. It was all Jared could do to get up every morning and care for his wife and children, much less pastor the Coastal congregation.

By this point, board members had started to receive comments from congregants, and they too could see what was happening. Jared simply was not able to fulfill the responsibilities of his position as senior pastor. While everyone had assumed this would be a relatively short-term issue, it was now clear that there may be no end in sight and that this might be the new normal for Jared and his family.

Members of the congregation and the board felt conflicted. They felt deep compassion for Jared and Melissa and wanted to do all they could to support the family. At the same time, things at church under Jared's responsibility were falling through the cracks. The church felt it needed a pastor who could be fully present. This was compounded by stagnant giving, which led some in the congregation to question whether keeping Jared constituted good stewardship when he wasn't able to perform the duties of his job. And yet it seemed like such a cruel thing to release a pastor for something out of his control and at his family's greatest time of need.

QUESTIONS FOR REFLECTION

1. With the information you've been given, how would you summarize the problem(s) in this case?

2. Who are the main characters and what are their roles in this situation?

3. What assumptions and values do you hear voiced by these characters?

4. What other information do you wish you had about this situation?

5. What seem to be the technical challenges involved in this case?

6. What are the adaptive challenges, and what type of adaptive challenges are they?

7. What risks and opportunities do you see in this case?

8. What biblical and theological principles should be considered in this case?

9. What are your suggested next steps for the parties involved?

10. What longer-term considerations might impact short-term decisions?

11. What work should be given "back to the people" here? To whom, and how?

12. What assumptions and values guide your recommended course of action?

13. What responses did you notice within yourself as you read this case?

14. Do you think anything could have been done differently, either individually or organizationally, to avoid this situation? If so, what?

15. Might this case be different if:

   a) Jared had not served at the church for so long or so faithfully?

   b) Jared served in a different position at the church instead of senior pastor?

   c) There were a potential end date to Melissa's health issues, even if two to three years out?

   d) Giving had not stalled, or if it had increased?

16. Issues to consider:

   a) What does an employee owe to its employer? What does an employer owe its employee? Is this different in churches and Christian ministries than in secular organizations?

   b) What does it look like to care well for a member of the congregation who is sick or hurting?

Commentary

Coastal Community Church seems to be in an unfortunate and uncomfortable bind. On the one hand, they love Jared and his family and want to support them. They are committed as a congregation to caring for their members who are sick and suffering. On the other hand, Jared is an employee, a leader, who has been hired to perform certain responsibilities. As Melissa's unknown illness drags on, it is uncertain whether Jared will be able to fulfill the requirements of his job. And frankly, Jared needs a break from the dual workload, but he and his family also desperately need the income and health insurance coverage provided by the church as his employer.

The leadership and congregation of Coastal will need to wrestle with this tension. Which is a greater priority: to care for the needs of the pastor and his family, or for the needs of the congregation and the church as employer? Are there creative solutions that would feel more like a win for everyone? Because right now, there seem to be no palatable options in sight.

ADDITIONAL QUESTIONS

1. Has your initial diagnosis of this situation changed? If so, how and why?

2. Which character(s) do you find yourself empathizing with?

3. Do you need to revise or address any of your assumptions?

Epilogue

Melissa's health problems continued. By this point, doctors were suggesting that she might spend the rest of her life bedridden, because no one had any answers. The family agonized over this prognosis. Jared loved pastoring. He did not want to let down or leave his church, but he also certainly did not want to neglect his wife. Meanwhile, within Coastal there grew an increasing sense that something needed to change, but there was still no clear solution.

The board of trustees decided to speak honestly with Jared. On the one hand, Jared understood. If he were in their position, he would likely feel the same concerns. On the other, it was hard for Jared not to feel abandoned by his church—the church that was not only his place of employment but his and his family's home—in his greatest time of need. Even though no decisions had been made, he felt increasing anxiety about what felt like a hopeless situation and even shame at his inability to fix it.

The leaders at Coastal decided to continue to wait out the situation. The church was big enough that it had staff members who could fill in the gaps for the foreseeable future. Jared was given freedom to come to work when he was able or to stay at home as needed. Meanwhile, Jared, Melissa, and the Coastal congregation, along with friends in the community and around the country, increased their prayers for the family.

Jared and his wife could sense the support. Jared had a new resolve to continue to serve his family and increased faith that God would provide, although he had no idea what that might look like. Melissa still felt miserable physically but also felt a new sense of peace in the midst of her great pain.

And then, all of a sudden, after almost two years of illness, Melissa started to get well. The changes were almost imperceptible at first, but week by week, the couple noticed them. Melissa was able to sit up in bed for some time each day and to sleep for a few uninterrupted hours each night. Her joint pain and swelling began to ease. Although she had very little muscle tone, she started to get out of bed, joining the family briefly for meals. Doctors were befuddled. They had never been able to diagnose the problem, and now they couldn't account for the improvement.

Over the next year, Melissa's health continued to steadily improve. She engaged in physical therapy to regain strength and full movement. In due time, she resumed standing, then walking, then driving, then cooking and caring for the house. Her and Jared's emotions flipped from tears of despair to tears of joy and astonishment, and the congregation was with them the entire way, rejoicing at every milestone.

As Melissa got better, Jared eventually resumed his full-time responsibilities at the church. He served for six more years after

Melissa's recovery before leaving to become lead pastor at a church located about an hour southeast of Coastal Community Church. Coastal continues its faithful presence in its community.

To this day, no one knows for certain what caused Melissa's illness or her recovery.

| Now What? |

1. How do you feel now that you've read the entire case and know how it ended?

2. Would you have acted similarly?

3. How could a different result have been achieved?

4. What actions can you, your fellow leaders, and your organization take to prepare for—and perhaps avoid, mitigate, or replicate—this particular situation or outcome?

Recommended Resources

Dyer, Dena. "How Can the Church Better Serve Those Suffering from Chronic Illness?" *The Better Samaritan* (blog), August 5, 2021, www.christianitytoday.com/better-samaritan/2021/august/how-can-church-better-serve-those-suffering-from-chronic-il.html.

Clergy Health Initiative at Duke Divinity School, https://divinity.duke.edu/initiatives/clergy-health-initiative.

CONCLUSION

As I mentioned in the introduction, every one of the cases in this book is drawn from real-life situations. Sometimes while I listened to and wrote these stories, I found myself shaking my head in disbelief. The variety of situations and the range and depth of the challenges experienced by the leaders in these stories underscore the complexity of ministry leadership in our day, not to mention the human fallenness that is just as pervasive in ministry as in the rest of the world.

And there are so many cases that were not included. The COVID-19 pandemic brought universal challenges and all sorts of creative responses and pivots. There are more and more cases emerging about new ways of doing church—although with many of those, the story is still being written. And there are situations which are personal challenges to leaders but not *leadership* challenges, per se. All of these are worthy of study and reflection, even if they did not make their way into this book. Perhaps someday in a sequel.

The cases in this book, while unique, reflect several common themes:

- Fear of conflict and reticence to address problems because of this fear.
- Unclear roles and structures of authority and power.

- Unclear strategies for decision-making.
- Conflicting expectations, values, or underlying assumptions.
- Cultural challenges, whether organizational, individual, generational, or other—or some combination.

As you take the cases in this book with you in your own leadership context, let me suggest two important principles along with several postures and next steps that can help you become more adept at adaptive leadership.

Principles

The foremost principle to remember is that *God's ways are not our ways*. In a number of the cases in this book, it is hard to tell whether things turned out well. We often want to assign blame, to easily identify the good guys and the bad guys, the winners and the losers. But when you examine more closely both the short- and long-term outcomes in these situations, it's not always cut and dried. Was an outcome the result of someone's good or bad decisions, or was it part of God's plan? Perhaps a short-term win had more serious long-term consequences, or God redeemed over time what seemed at first glance to be a loss. Thankfully God has an eternal, kingdom perspective and can redeem human failings, because we certainly have plenty of them.

The second principle is that *you are not alone*. As we have seen in these pages, adaptive challenges are found in any ministry leadership context: church or parachurch, large or small, old or new, urban, suburban, or rural. Right now, as you read this, someone, somewhere, is seeking to lead through an adaptive challenge. While the details of your situation may be unique, others have navigated similar situations, simply based on the common themes. And as our world becomes increasingly complex, the number and complexity of adaptive challenges will similarly increase. Leadership in these environments is hard and often lonely. Therefore, find others who have been there, *are* there, and can support you on the journey. These fellow travelers can be a tremendous resource for both leadership expertise and personal encouragement.

Postures

I would suggest that the most critical posture for an adaptive leader is *humility*. This character trait and fruit of the Spirit can be described as "the modest perception of one's own significance."[1] It means thinking more highly of others, not in a self-denigrating way but realizing that we do not know it all and can learn from many other sources. This posture actually runs counter to some leadership philosophies and perhaps to our own expectations that a leader should always have all the answers.

Humility is reflected in two subpostures: *learning* and *listening*. By learning I mean not only reading books, listening to podcasts, and filling our heads with knowledge. Being a learner also includes assessing our practical skills and spiritual, emotional, and relational health; acknowledging reality; and being willing to—even seeking to—continually grow. Are you willing to acknowledge your shortcomings, to broaden your perspective, to change your mind? Rick Warren, founding pastor of Saddleback Church, has said that "if you stop learning, you stop leading," and I heartily concur. Learning is a part of the ongoing growth that is required for continued effectiveness as a leader.

Closely related to learning is the posture of listening. This,

---

1. Sarah Kristenson, "Eleven Ways to Practice Humility throughout Your Life," Happier Human, October 14, 2021, www.happierhuman.com/practice-humility/.

again, involves not just cognitive intake or assent. It requires true presence: to what, whom, or Whom we are listening, to what is going on within ourselves, and to what is happening in the "space between" in the room. This posture also goes against the contemporary model of leadership and the trend toward platform-building, which favor talking, telling, even shouting. Are you willing to use your ears more than your mouth and to hear and take in what someone is saying, instead of just awaiting your turn to talk or running what they say through your judgment filter?

Next Steps

In addition to developing the postures of humility, learning, and listening, you can take several next steps to develop your and your organization's adaptive leadership capacity and ability.

First, you can look at the themes from the cases in this book and assess whether any of these are problem areas in your leadership context:

- Is there fear of conflict, and how does this play out? If there is, what can be done to minimize this fear and cultivate a climate that works conflict to the surface in healthy ways?
- Do you have clear roles and structures of authority and power? If not, where are the gaps and what needs to be clarified or better communicated?
- Do you have clear strategies for decision-making? If not, where do these need to be shored up?
- Are there clear and shared expectations, values, and underlying assumptions? If not, where are the tension points? Are there unspoken expectations and assumptions that need to be clarified and verbalized?

- What are the cultural challenges or disconnects in
  your context that you may not have thought about?
  Think about not only ethnicity but also age, gender,
  socioeconomics, level of education, and others.

Second, you can apply the Questions for Reflection from
each chapter to the challenges you are facing in your own context. For example:

- Are the challenges in your situation technical or adaptive?
- What are the assumptions and values of the people in
  your context?
- What risks and opportunities do you see?
- What biblical and theological principles should be
  considered?
- What work should be given "back to the people"?
- What are your assumptions and values?
- What emotions do you recognize within yourself in
  response to the situation?

Third, you can work on your ability to "get on the balcony,"
to see the big picture and reflect even in the middle of the action.

Leadership is a gift, a skill, and an art. Whether or not you
consider yourself naturally gifted as a leader, adaptive leadership
is a skill that can be learned and developed. And with enough
practice, it can truly become a work of art: of ascertaining the
real issues, of knowing how much pressure or relief to apply and
when, and of engaging and motivating people throughout the
system to perform the work required to navigate the challenge.

As you go forth and navigate the uncharted territory on
your leadership journey, may you do so with wisdom, grace, and
courage.

ACKNOWLEDGMENTS

As with any book, the author's name is on the cover, but it is really a group project. I'd like to thank everyone who has played a part in bringing this project to life and encouraging me along the way.

First, thank you to those who have shared their stories with me for this book. Many of these leaders have weathered excruciating experiences. I pray that your willingness to share has brought you additional insight and even healing and that your stories will help many others grow in their leadership. In alphabetical order:

Craig Blomberg   Steve McCord   Rowland Smith
Kimmy Dowdy   Chantel Pagan   Tyler Thompson
Kathryn Helleman   Marshall Shelley   Scott Wenig
Alan Henderson   Brett Sleasman

And also those who have chosen to remain anonymous but whose contributions are no less significant.

Thanks to my doctor of ministry students at Denver Seminary, who teach me just as much as I teach them about ministry and leadership. It's an honor to walk with you and learn from you on this unique road that is doctoral studies. Thanks also to my incredible colleagues at Denver Seminary, who sharpen me every day. It's a gift to do work you love with people you love.

Thanks to Tod Bolsinger for the inspiration for the title from his excellent work *Canoeing the Mountains: Christian Leadership in Uncharted Territory*. He has blazed a trail with his book that I have endeavored to follow with mine.

Thank you to my agent, Keely Boeving, and to Greg Johnson and the team at WordServe Literary. I have learned that the way you care for your authors is a rare gift, and I am fortunate to be part of the WordServe family.

Thanks to Rick Dunn and Harv Powers for our Nile Mastermind and for being my steadfast champions and encouragers. It is a rich grace to journey with people who know you so deeply.

Thank you to Kyle Rohane, my acquisitions editor at Zondervan Reflective (and, I must add, a fellow Denver Seminary alum). It has been a privilege to work with you from your time at CT Pastors to now, and I hope for more opportunities to do so down the road. And thanks to the Zondervan Reflective team that brought this book to life, including Brian Phipps, Tammy Johnson, Alexis De Weese, Amy Bigler, and Kent Hendricks.

Thank you, Marshall Shelley, for that first invitation to write for *Leadership Journal* many years ago, and then for the invitation to join you on staff at Denver Seminary. Working for you and with you has been an absolute delight, and I will be forever grateful and indebted to you for your trust and support.

Thanks to the faculty, staff, and students at Ridley College in Cambridge, England, for your hospitality during my personal retreat in May 2022. It was a joy to participate in your community and to see what God is doing in his church across the pond when I wasn't hunched over my laptop in the library, working on this manuscript.

And last but never least, thank you to my husband, David, who has been my best friend and biggest cheerleader for close to thirty years and counting. We've got a pretty amazing thing going, don't we!? All my love, always.

BIBLIOGRAPHY

Allison, Gregg R. "Part Four: The Government of the Church." In *Sojourners and Strangers: The Doctrine of the Church*. Wheaton, IL: Crossway, 2012.

Anderson, Robert J., and William A. Adams. *Scaling Leadership: Building Organizational Capability and Capacity to Create Outcomes That Matter Most*. Hoboken, NJ: Wiley, 2019.

Annan, Kent. *You Welcomed Me: Loving Refugees and Immigrants because God First Loved Us*. Downers Grove, IL: InterVarsity Press, 2018.

Baker, Mark D. *Centered-Set Church: Discipleship and Community without Judgmentalism*. Downers Grove, IL: IVP Academic, 2022.

Bird, Michael, and Brian Rosner, eds. *Mending a Fractured Church: How to Seek Unity with Integrity*. Bellingham, WA: Lexham Press, 2015.

Black, Amy E., gen. ed. *Five Views on the Church and Politics*. Counterpoints: Bible and Theology. Grand Rapids: Zondervan Academic, 2015.

Bolman, Lee G., and Terrence E. Deal. *Reframing Organizations: Artistry, Choice, and Leadership*. 7th ed. San Francisco: Jossey-Bass, 2021.

Bolsinger, Tod. *Canoeing the Mountains: Christian Leadership in Uncharted Territory*. Downers Grove, IL: InterVarsity Press, 2018.

Brand, Chad Owen, and R. Stanton Norm, eds. *Perspectives on Church Government: Five Views of Church Polity*. Nashville: B&H Academic, 2004.

Bridges, William. *Managing Transitions: Making the Most of Change.* 25th anniv. ed. Boston: Da Capo Press, 2017.

Campolo, Tony, and Bart Campolo. *Why I Left, Why I Stayed: Conversations on Christianity between an Evangelical Father and His Humanist Son.* New York: HarperOne, 2018.

Christensen, Clayton M. *The Innovator's Dilemma: When New Technologies Cause Great Firms to Fail.* Management of Innovation and Change. Boston: Harvard Business Review Press, 2015.

Church Law and Tax (website), www.churchlawandtax.com.

Cladis, George. *Leading the Team-Based Church: How Pastors and Church Staffs Can Grow Together into a Powerful Fellowship of Leaders.* San Francisco: Jossey-Bass, 1999.

Clergy Health Initiative at Duke Divinity School, https://divinity.duke.edu/initiatives/clergy-health-initiative.

Cloud, Henry. *Necessary Endings: The Employees, Businesses, and Relationships That All of Us Have to Give Up in Order to Move Forward.* New York: HarperCollins, 2011.

Covey, Stephen M. R. *The Speed of Trust: The One Thing That Changes Everything.* New York: Free Press, 2006.

Cymbala, Jim. *Fresh Wind, Fresh Fire: What Happens When God's Spirit Invades the Hearts of His People.* Updated and expanded. Grand Rapids: Zondervan, 2018.

DeGroat, Chuck. *When Narcissism Comes to Church: Healing Your Community from Emotional and Spiritual Abuse.* Downers Grove, IL: InterVarsity Press, 2022.

Diagnostic and Statistical Manual of Mental Disorders. 5th ed. Washington, DC: American Psychiatric Publishing, Inc., 2013.

Duck, Jeanie Daniel. *The Change Monster: The Human Forces That Fuel or Foil Corporate Transformation and Change.* New York: Three Rivers Press, 2001.

Dyer, Dena. "How Can the Church Better Serve Those Suffering from Chronic Illness?" *The Better Samaritan* (blog), August 5, 2021, www.christianitytoday.com/better-samaritan/2021/august/how-can-church-better-serve-those-suffering-from-chronic-il.html.

Ellet, William. *The Case Study Handbook: How to Read, Discuss, and Write Persuasively about Cases*. Boston: Harvard Business Review Press, 2007.

Ellis, Lynne, and Doug Fields. *Mission Trips from Start to Finish: How to Organize and Lead Impactful Mission Trips*. Loveland, CO: Group Publishing, 2008.

Evangelical Council for Financial Accountability. "ECFA's Integrity Standards for Nonprofits," www.ecfa.org/Standards.aspx.

Grenny, Joseph, Kerry Patterson, Ron McMillan, Al Switzler, and Emily Gregory. *Crucial Conversations: Tools for Talking When Stakes Are High*. 3rd ed. New York: McGraw Hill, 2022.

Hagberg, Janet O., and Robert A. Guelich: *The Critical Journey: Stages in the Life of Faith*. 2nd ed. Salem, WI: Sheffield Publishing Co., 2004.

Hagley, Scott. *Eat What Is Set before You: A Missiology of the Congregation in Context*. Skyforest, CA: Urban Loft Publishers, 2019.

Hammar, Richard R. *Church Governance: What Leaders Must Know to Conduct Legally Sound Church Business*. Carol Stream, IL: Christianity Today International, 2019.

Hanberg, Erik. *The Little Book of Boards: A Board Member's Handbook for Small (and Very Small) Nonprofits*. North Charleston, SC: CreateSpace, 2015.

Heifetz, Ronald A. *Leadership without Easy Answers*. Cambridge, MA: Harvard University Press, 1994.

Henderson, Daniel. *Glorious Finish: Keeping Your Eye on the Prize of Eternity in a Time of Pastoral Failings*. Chicago: Moody, 2020.

Herrington, Jim, Mike Bonem, and James H. Furr. *Leading Congregational Change: A Practical Guide for the Transformational Journey*. Minneapolis: Fortress Press, 2000.

Herrington, Jim, Trisha Taylor, and R. Robert Creech. *The Leader's Journey: Accepting the Call to Personal and Congregational Transformation*. 2nd ed. Grand Rapids: Baker Academic, 2020.

Hoover, Sharon R. *Mapping Church Missions: A Compass for Ministry Strategy*. Downers Grove, IL: InterVarsity Press, 2018.

House, Brad, and Gregg Allison. *MultiChurch: Exploring the Future of Multisite.* Grand Rapids: Zondervan, 2017.

Johnson, Andy. *Missions: How the Local Church Goes Global.* Wheaton, IL: Crossway, 2017.

Kendrick, Klint C. *The HR Practitioner's Guide to Cultural Integration in Mergers and Acquisitions: Overcoming Culture Clash to Drive M&A Deal Value.* Mergers and Acquisitions Roundtable, 2022.

Kimble, Jeremy M. *Forty Questions about Church Membership and Discipline.* Forty Questions. Grand Rapids: Kregel Academic, 2017.

Kotter, John. *Accelerate: Building Strategic Agility for a Faster-Moving World.* Boston: Harvard Business Review Press, 2014.

Kotter, John P. *Leading Change.* Boston: Harvard Business Review Press, 2012.

Kraaijenbrink, Jeroen. "What Does VUCA Really Mean?" *Forbes,* December 19, 2018, www.forbes.com/sites/jeroenkraaijenbrink /2018/12/19/what-does-vuca-really-mean/?sh=5b8318bd17d6.

Leeman, Jonathan. *Church Membership: How the World Knows Who Represents Jesus.* 9Marks: Building Healthy Churches. Wheaton, IL: Crossway, 2012.

Lencioni, Patrick. *The Advantage: Why Organizational Health Trumps Everything Else in Business.* San Francisco: Jossey-Bass, 2012.

Lewis, Robert, and Wayne Cordeiro. *Culture Shift: Transforming Your Church from the Inside Out.* San Francisco: Jossey-Bass, 2005.

Lewis, Tracy. *How to Write Articles, Constitutions, and Bylaws for Churches.* Independently published, 2019.

Lingenfelter, Sherwood. *Leading Cross-Culturally: Covenant Relationships for Effective Christian Leadership.* Grand Rapids: Baker Academic, 2008.

MacDonald, Gordon. *Rebuilding Your Broken World.* Nashville: Thomas Nelson, 2004.

Mandes, Alejandro. *The New Samaria: Opening Our Eyes to Our Multiethnic Future.* Colorado Springs, CO: NavPress, 2021.

McIntosh, Gary L., and Samuel D. Rima. *Overcoming the Dark Side of Leadership: How to Become an Effective Leader by Confronting Potential Failures.* Grand Rapids: Baker, 2007.

McKnight, Scot, and Laura Barringer. *A Church Called TOV: Forming a Goodness Culture That Resists Abuses of Power and Promotes Healing.* Carol Stream, IL: Tyndale Momentum, 2020.

Mesa, Ivan, ed. *Before You Lose Your Faith: Deconstructing Doubt in the Church.* Deerfield, IL: Gospel Coalition, 2021.

Northouse, Peter G. *Leadership Theory and Practice.* 9th ed. Newbury Park, CA: Sage Publishing, Inc., 2021.

Ortlund, Dane. *Gentle and Lowly: The Heart of Christ for Sinners and Sufferers.* Wheaton, IL: Crossway, 2020.

Parker, Marsha. *Shared Governance for Beginners: Six Competencies for a Quick Start.* Shared Governance Practitioner. North Charleston, SC: CreateSpace, 2016.

Quinn, Robert E. *Deep Change: Discovering the Leader Within.* San Francisco: Jossey-Bass, 1996.

Rothwell, William. *Effective Succession Planning: Ensuring Leadership Continuity and Building Talent from Within.* 5th ed. New York: AMACOM, 2015.

Schein, Edgar H. *Organizational Culture and Leadership.* 5th ed. Hoboken, NJ: Wiley, 2016.

Senge, Peter M. *The Fifth Discipline: The Art and Practice of the Learning Organization.* New York: Currency, 2006.

Shaw, Haydn. *Sticking Points: How to Get Five Generations Working Together in the Twelve Places They Come Apart.* Carol Stream, IL: Tyndale Momentum, 2020.

Shelley, Marshall. *Ministering to Problem People in Your Church: What to Do with Well-Intentioned Dragons.* Minneapolis: Bethany, 2013.

Strong, Mark E. *Who Moved My Neighborhood? Leading Congregations through Gentrification and Economic Change.* Downers Grove, IL: InterVarsity Press, 2022.

Tomberlin, Jim, and Warren Bird. *Better Together: Making Church Mergers Work.* Expanded and updated. Minneapolis: Fortress, 2020.

Two Loops Model of Systemic Change, www.youtube.com/watch?v=LQWKmtx8L2s.

Vanderbloemen, William, and Warren Bird. *Next: Pastoral Succession That Works*. Grand Rapids: Baker, 2014.

Van der Kolk, Bessel. *The Body Keeps the Score: Brain, Mind, and Body in the Healing of Trauma*. New York: Penguin, 2014.

Van Yperen, Jim. *Making Peace: A Guide to Overcoming Church Conflict*. Chicago: Moody, 2002.

Vaters, Karl. *Small Church Essentials: Field-Tested Principles for Leading a Healthy Congregation of under 250*. Chicago: Moody, 2018.

Ward, Angie, gen. ed. *Kingdom and Country: Following Jesus in the Land That You Love*. Kingdom Conversations. Colorado Springs, CO: NavPress, 2022.

Ward, Angie, gen. ed. *When the Universe Cracks: Living as God's People in Times of Crisis*. Colorado Springs, CO: NavPress, 2021.

Watkins, Michael D. *The First Ninety Days: Proven Strategies for Getting up to Speed Faster and Smarter*. Boston: Harvard Business Review Press, 2013.

Whitehead, Andrew. *Taking America Back for God: Christian Nationalism in the United States*. Oxford: Oxford Univ. Press, 2020.

Woolverton, David E. *Mission Rift: Leading through Church Conflict*. Minneapolis: Fortress, 2021.

TOPICAL INDEX